A CENTURY
OF
STEAM
TRAINS

BROCKHAMPTON PRESS

First published in Great Britain by Brockhampton Press
a member of
the Hodder Headline Group
20 Bloomsbury Street
London WC1B 3QA

ISBN 1 86019 796 5

Designed and produced by
Superlaunch Ltd
PO Box 207, Abingdon
Oxfordshire OX13 6TA, England
Colour separation by Svoboda,
Prague
Printed and bound in the UAE

CONTENTS

INTRODUCTION

For many centuries man had appreciated the advantages that were to be gained by running wheeled vehicles, especially those carrying heavy loads, on relatively smooth rails rather than over rough and uneven ground. Some illustrations had appeared as early as 1550 of wagonways used in German mines, and during the next 200 years their use became common in mines all over Europe. In Britain, especially, they were used to ferry coal from the mines to nearby rivers and, later, to the canals. For many years the wagons were hauled over wooden rails, the wheels of the wagons being grooved or flanged for guidance. Later on, iron plating was added to prolong the life of the rails; towards the end of the eighteenth century cast iron plates, usually laid on stone blocks and formed with flanges to guide plain wheels, became more common.

At about the same time, other users began to experiment with iron rails, which were intended for use with flanged wheels, rather than plates. The next step was the introduction of wrought iron, which enabled much longer rails to be used. A system of rolling lengths of wrought iron of uniform cross-section was patented in 1820, and from these ultimately the modern forms of railway track were to be evolved.

The construction of canals for use in transporting freight was an expensive business, for use where navigable rivers did not exist. By the beginning of the nineteenth century there were many schemes for long-distance railways, primarily at the instigation of the mine owners.

In 1801 a significant step was taken when an Act of Parliament authorised the Surrey Iron Railway to carry traffic over the 14.5km (9 miles) between Croydon and the River Thames at Wandsworth. This line was the first officially-sanctioned public railway, and opened in 1803.

However, as long as the wagons were drawn by horses there were practical limits on the weight and speed of traffic that such railways would be able to

Cugnot demonstrating his steam car to the Marquis de Monteynard, the French Minister for War, in 1771

carry. The steam engines that had become increasingly common by the end of the eighteenth century seemed to offer a promising source of power. As early as 1769, Nicolas Cugnot had built a steam carriage in Paris, only to be imprisoned for his pains. By the time the Surrey Iron Railway was operating an English engineer, Richard Trevithick, had produced his first steam-propelled vehicle for use on the roads.

Trevithick, the son of a mine engineer from Cornwall in the west of England, built a successful steam carriage in 1801. This was significant because it incorporated a return flue to heat the water in the boiler. He went on to build a second carriage, followed by a locomotive which was designed to run on the plateway between the Pen-y-Darren ironworks in South Wales, and a local canal. On 21 February 1804 Trevithick's locomotive hauled 10.16 tonnes (10 tons) of iron as well as a

Richard Trevithick's locomotive, built for the Pen-y-Darren ironworks near Merthyr Tydfil, South Wales. It was the first locomotive to haul a load successfully, on 13 February 1804

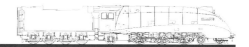

number of passengers for the length of the 16.1km (10 miles) plateway, though only at the cost of heavy damage to the iron plates.

This pioneer locomotive employed a single horizontal cylinder with a large flywheel and the wheels being driven through a system of gears. His later locomotive of 1808, *Catch-me-who-can*, used a vertical cylinder to drive the wheels by means of connecting rods.

In 1805 Trevithick built another engine, this time for the Wylam colliery. The engine, like his earlier Pen-y-Darren model, proved to be too heavy for the plateway. However, it was this locomotive that was to inspire a number of local mine engineers to experiment with the building of others. The most important of these early pioneers was George Stephenson.

Although barely literate, Stephenson was a visionary genius of mechanics, who not only perfected the basic pattern on which all future steam locomotives were to be based, but also foresaw the creation of a national railway network. Each of his locomotives embodied several further improvements on Trevithick's original pattern: his first was the *Blücher*, of 1814. This had flanged wheels to run on rails rather than plates, and in subsequent engines he perfected a direct drive from the cylinders via connecting rods to the driving wheels.

When he became involved in the planning of the Stockton & Darlington

Richard Trevithick's 1808 locomotive, Catch-me-who-can, *on demonstration in London*

Railway, Stephenson adopted wrought-iron I-section rails mounted on stone blocks. His first locomotive for the new railway, the *Locomotion*, used rods rather than chains to connect the two pairs of wheels.

The opening of the Stockton & Darlington Railway on 27 September 1825 was a historic occasion, making the first use of steam power on a public railway. The locomotives themselves were still temperamental, however,

being subject to boiler explosions and broken wheels.

By this time George Stephenson had become the acknowledged expert on all matters related to both railways and locomotives, and he was invited to advise on the construction and on the operation of a projected railway between Liverpool and Manchester.

In order to find the best locomotive for railway use, a series of trials were held at Rainhill in October 1829, and the undoubted star of the contest was the *Rocket*, built by the firm which George Stephenson had founded and of which his son Robert was the head.

Richard Trevithick 1771–1833 *George Stephenson 1781–1848* *Robert Stephenson 1803–1859*

PUFFING BILLY 0-4-0

William Hedley's Puffing Billy *of 1813. It was used for half a century at a Northumbrian colliery and is now preserved at the Science Museum, London*

Country of origin: UK
Railway: Wylam Colliery
Date: 1813
Length overall: not known
Total weight: not known
Cylinders: two 229 x 914mm (9 x 36in)
Driving wheels: 0.99m (3ft 3in)
Axle load: not known
Grate area: 0.56m² (6.03sqft)

Water: not known
Heating surface: 7.15m² (76.96sq ft)
Superheater: none
Steam pressure: 3.3kg/cm² (47psi)
Adhesive weight: not known
Tractive force: 1,410kg (3,100lb)

John Blenkinsop was superintendent of the Middleton Railway, which was a colliery railway near Leeds, England. It was his contention that the ability of a wheel to push itself along a smooth rail was insufficient, and thus he had his rails built with rack teeth alongside their surfaces.

William Hedley, the manager of Wylam Colliery near Newcastle, disagreed with Blenkinsop's view. After much demonstration of the matter on paper, in 1813 Hedley had built two locomotives, *Puffing Billy* and *Wylam Dilly*. These each had their cranks on a jack shaft, which in turn was geared to two pairs of driving wheels. Hedley's technique has been employed ever since.

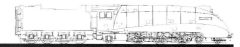

LOCOMOTION 0–4–0

Country of origin: UK
Railway: Stockton & Darlington Railway (S&D)
Date: 1825
Length overall: 7.31m (24ft)
Total weight: 6,700kg (14,774lb)
Cylinders: two 241 x 610mm (9.5 x 24in)
Driving wheels: 1.22m (4ft)
Axle load: not known
Grate area: 0.6m² (6.46sq ft)
Water: not known
Heating surface: 5.56m² (60sq ft)
Superheater: none
Steam pressure: 1.75kg/cm² (25psi)
Adhesive weight: 6,700kg (14,774lb)
Tractive force: 580kg (1,280lb)

This was the locomotive that inaugurated the Stockton & Darlington Railway in September 1825, which was the first public railway to have steam traction. *Locomotion* was also the first engine to be built at the new workshops of Robert Stephenson & Co. With its cast-iron wheels and a pair of

No 1 Locomotion was delivered in September 1825 from Stephenson's Forth Street works in Newcastle. Its wrought-iron boiler was 3.15m (10ft 4in) long and 1.22m (4ft) across

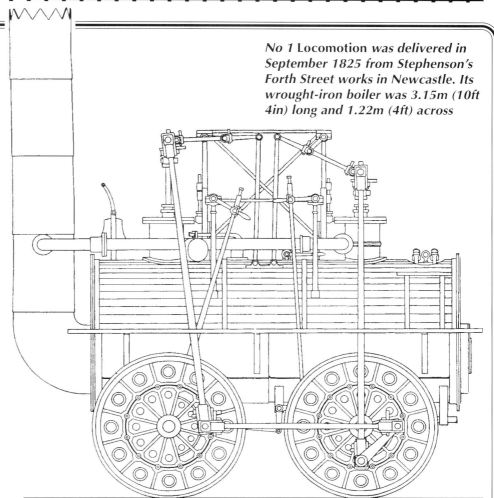

cylinders, it weighed 6.7 tonnes (6.6 tons). On the railway's opening day, *Locomotion* was able to haul, albeit rather slowly, a 69-tonne (67.9-ton) train of 28 wagons. Difficulties in steam production imposed restrictions in ordinary use, and it had a troubled existence. Despite suffering a broken wheel within one month of entering service and a boiler explosion in 1828, however, it remained in traffic until 1840.

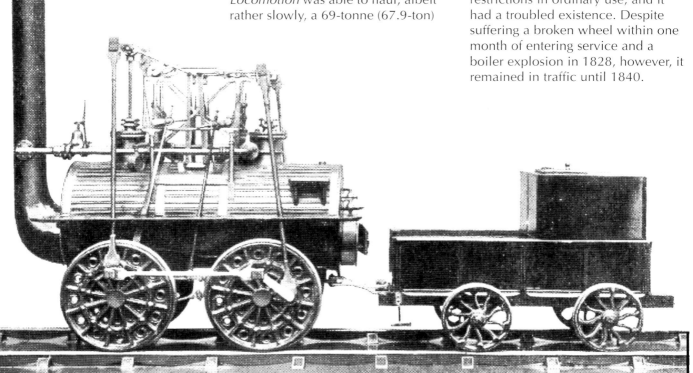

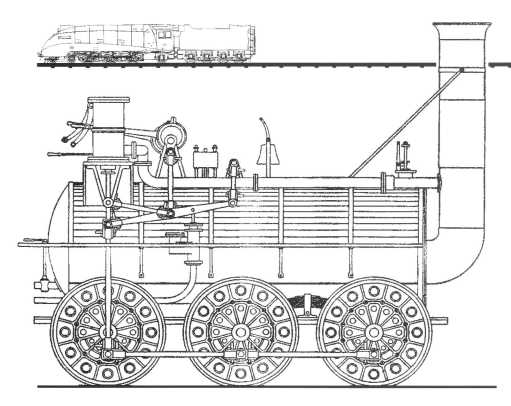

The essential features of the *Rocket*, which were to endure throughout the development of the steam locomotive, were the multi-tube boiler and the blast pipe. Hot gases from the fire passed through the fire tubes in the boiler, heating the water to produce steam. The steam was fed to the cylinders, where by acting on the pistons it drove the wheels. It was then exhausted through a blast pipe in the chimney to create the draught on the fire.

By the time that the Liverpool & Manchester Railway (L&M) was ready to begin operations in September 1830, news of the new steam railways was arousing widespread interest. Across the Atlantic, where settlement of the fertile river valleys in the interior of the United States was getting under way, the growing population was in need of improved communications.

The response of the east-coast cities, once New York had secured the first water route to the Great Lakes, was to

Above: *the* **Royal George,** *built by* **Timothy Hackworth** *in September 1827 for the Stockton & Darlington Railway. It had a 3.96m (13ft) boiler with a 1.32m (4ft 4in) diameter, and* *a heating surface more than twice that of* Locomotion *at 13.1m² (141sq ft)*

Below: *the opening of the L&M Railway on 15 September 1830*

THE ROCKET 0–2–2

Country of origin: UK
Railway: Liverpool & Manchester Railway (L&M)
Date: 1829
Length overall: 6.55m (21ft 6in)
Total weight: 4,545kg (10,000lb)
Cylinders: two 203 x 419mm (8 x 16.5in)
Driving wheels: 1.435m (4ft 8.5in)
Axle load: not known
Grate area: 0.56m² (6.03sq ft)
Water: not known
Heating surface: 13.28m² (142.95sq ft)
Steam pressure: 3.5kg/cm² (50psi)
Adhesive weight: 2,500kg (5,512lb)
Tractive force: 622kg (1,370lb)

Built in 1829 by George and Robert Stephenson, *Rocket* is the world's most famous steam locomotive; and rightly so, because its design marked the transition from the pioneers' efforts to the modern steam engine.

The *Rocket* was designed specifically for the Rainhill Trials that took place on 6 October 1829, and incorporated the latest thinking of its builders. It was based on experiments carried out with the *Lancashire Witch* during the previous year, but with the addition of a water-tube boiler, which had 25 tubes through the barrel. The firebox and grate were separated from, and placed under, the rear of the boiler. Exhaust steam was used as

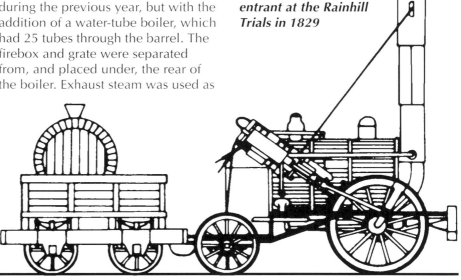

Stephenson's Rocket, *with its wooden tender, was the successful entrant at the Rainhill Trials in 1829*

a blast up the chimney to force the fire.

The Stephensons adopted a light single-driver design, with two cylinders mounted at a 35-degree angle. The working weight of the locomotive was 4.3 tonnes (4.23 tons), and at the Trials *Rocket* reached a speed of 48km/h (30mph) while hauling a load of 12.9 tonnes (12.7 tons).

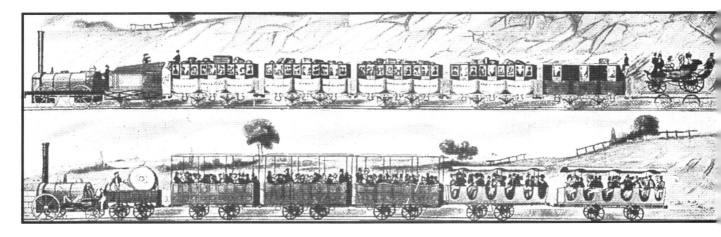

Above: *early trains on the Liverpool & Manchester Railway, in 1830*

look for their own means of communication. As the mountain ranges formed a formidable obstacle to building canals, a number of cities turned to railways as a possible solution.

The first in the race was Baltimore, and in February 1828 the Maryland state legislature chartered the Baltimore & Ohio Railroad (B&O), an ambitious scheme for a 611.8km (380-mile) railway that would connect with the Ohio River at Wheeling. Work was begun on 4 July 1829, and by the following year horses were hauling rail cars over the first 20.9km (13 miles) of track.

Below: *Sharp, Roberts & Co's engine* Experiment *was delivered to the Liverpool & Manchester Railway in 1833*

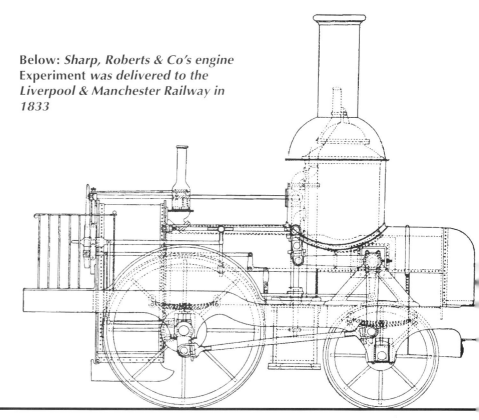

Bottom: Planet *hauling a passenger train across a stone bridge on the Liverpool & Manchester Railway, 1830*

STOURBRIDGE LION 0–4–0

Country of origin: USA
Railway: Delaware & Hudson Canal Company (D&H)
Date: 1829
Length overall: 3.924m (12ft 10.5in)
Total weight: not known
Cylinders: two 215 x 914mm (8.5 x 36in)
Driving wheels: 1.24m (4ft 1in)
Axle load: 3,920kg (8,624lb)
Grate area: not known
Water: not known
Heating surface: not known
Superheater: none
Steam pressure: not known
Adhesive weight: 7,127kg (15,680lb) excluding tender

The *Stourbridge Lion* was the first steam locomotive ever to run commercially in America. It was one of the first four English-built locomotives ever sent to America, and the only one about which anything is known.

It arrived in New York by sailing vessel on 13 May 1829. Driven by Horatio Allen, the young civil engineer of the Delaware & Hudson Canal Company (D&H), the engine made a trial run along 4.8km (three miles) of railway which included a

Foster & Rastrick's* Stourbridge Lion *was the first steam locomotive ever to run commercially in the United States, in 1829. The locomotive is now exhibited at the Smithsonian Institution, Washington DC

bridge on a curve of 102m (112yd) radius, at Honesdale, Pennsylvania, on 8 August 1829. The trial was a success, but the locomotive was found to be too heavy for the track, and was relegated to shunting duty in the coal yards of the D&H before being converted to stationary use.

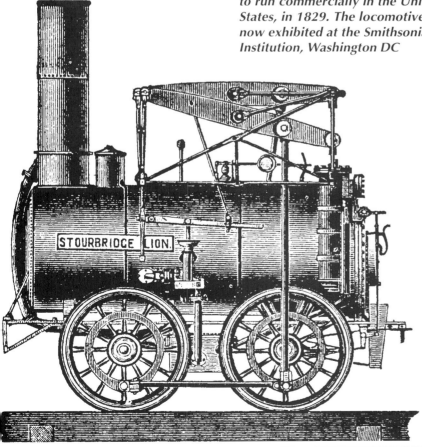

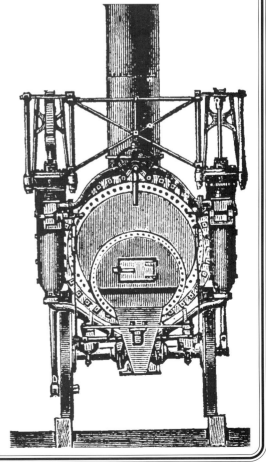

A steam locomotive had been tested in the United States already, as a result of the Delaware & Hudson Canal Company having sent Horatio Allen to observe the Rainhill Trials. Following on that event, he had ordered four locomotives built, one from Robert Stephenson and the rest from the Stourbridge firm of Foster & Rastrick. One of the latter company's locomotives, the *Stourbridge Lion*, made the first steam locomotive trip in America on 8 August 1829. A year later the *Tom Thumb* was built by one of the B&O shareholders, Peter Cooper, and tested on the B&O's track between Baltimore and Ellicott's Mills. *Tom Thumb* pulled a coach carrying 32 passengers at speeds of up to 29km/h (18mph) on 28 August 1830.

In order to develop the potential of this new form of transport, the railroad offered prizes for the best locomotives entered in a competition which was to be held on 1 June 1831. Only one locomotive was able to meet the conditions of the competition. This was the *York*,

Below: Tom Thumb *was built by Peter Cooper at his own expense. It had a vertical boiler and two vertical cylinders. Tom Thumb *was

the first locomotive in the United States to haul a wagon loaded with passengers

built by Phineas Davis, and as a result the Baltimore & Ohio ordered twenty examples of what later became known as Davis's grasshopper engines. The first of these was named *Atlantic*, and

Below: *the first stone was laid on the Baltimore & Ohio Railroad, America's pioneer railway, on 4 July 1828*

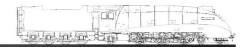

*Below: a replica of the Baltimore &
Ohio Railroad's Atlantic, which was
the first of the Phineas Davis
grasshopper locomotives to be built
after his successful York*

Above: John Bull *was the first steam
locomotive to run on rails in the
United States. However, it was never
put to practical use and the first
commercial American locomotives
were British-built*

several of the class served the railroad
for over 50 years.

By this time, other cities had followed
Baltimore's lead and railroads were
being built westwards from Boston,
Philadelphia, Richmond, Charleston
and Savannah. Within a few years,
others were started to connect the
inland cities with the lakes, rivers and
seas that still formed the main long-
distance transport routes, and new
firms were building locomotives to
operate on them. By the middle of the
nineteenth century, the United States
had the biggest rail network in the
world, and it was the railways that went
on to transform the republic.

Meanwhile the nations of Europe
were able to make better and quicker
progress with industrialisation as the
railways developed. The first railway
built in France was opened between
Andrézieux-Bouthéon and St Etienne in
1828, though steam traction was not
introduced until 1832 on a new line
from St Etienne to Lyons. New lines
followed in Germany and Belgium in
1835, and by the end of the decade
steam railways were also in operation
in Ireland, Austria, the Netherlands and
Italy. Other countries followed suit
during the 1840s. These usually relied
on locomotives built by Stephenson or
other English constructors to begin
with, but national characteristics soon
became apparent as indigenous designs
were produced, many of them with
specific innovations introduced to meet
domestic requirements of either terrain
or of haulage.

One consequence of the initial use
of Stephenson locomotives was the

widespread adoption of Stephenson's
standard gauge of 1.435m (4ft 8.5in).
This was selected in the first place for
no better reason than that it happened
to be the gauge used by the mine
railway where Stephenson's first
experiments had been carried out.
Eventually the benefits of uniformity
outweighed the drawbacks of the
restricted width, and only Russia,
Finland, Spain and Portugal chose
different gauges. Consequently, it was
soon possible to run international trains
through most of Europe.

Another important characteristic of
the continental railways was the large
measure of governmental control that
was exercised over their location. In the
United States and in Britain many
competing lines were built, and it was
some years before even the gauge was
standardised on a national basis. On
the other hand, elsewhere in Europe the
tendency was for national governments

to license private companies to build
along selected routes, or to undertake
the construction themselves, thus
avoiding a good deal of the wasteful
competition that was to mar the
development of both the British and
American systems.

In 1837 the Grand Junction Railway
was opened between Warrington and
Birmingham, to complete the first trunk
route between the latter city and
Liverpool and Manchester. Both of the
Stephensons were involved, George being
engaged on the Grand Junction and his
son, Robert, also busy on the major
route from Birmingham to London.

By the end of the nineteenth century,
the majority of the small lines that had
appeared early in the development of
the railway system in Britain had been
consolidated into a number of larger
companies. All of these developed their
own characteristic styles, which were
reflected in the architecture of their
stations, the pattern of their services
and, most visibly, in the brightly-
painted locomotives.

Below: *Marc Séguin's locomotive,
which hauled the first French steam
train on the St Etienne to Lyons
railway in 1830*

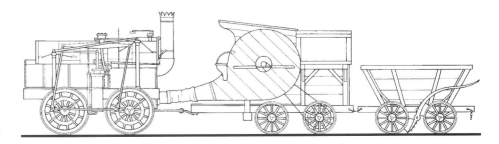

European Locomotive Development 1830–1855

LIVERPOOL 0–4–0

Country of origin: UK
Railway: Liverpool & Manchester
Railway (L&M)
Date: 1830

*Bury, Curtis & Kennedy's 0–4–0
engine* Liverpool, *which was tried on
the Liverpool & Manchester Railway
in July 1830, was the first engine to
have inside horizontal cylinders and
a crank axle, in advance
even of Stephenson's*
Planet *in these respects.*
Liverpool *had 1.83m
(6ft) coupled wheels
and 305 x 457mm
(12 x 18in) cylinders,
which were inclined
slightly upwards
to allow the piston
rods to pass underneath
the leading axle*

Edward Bury originally intended to
run this locomotive in the Rainhill
Trials, but it was not ready in time.
He finally delivered his inside-
cylinder four-wheeler to the Liverpool
& Manchester Railway in 1830. It
was a variant on Stephenson's *Planet*
type of locomotive, and both

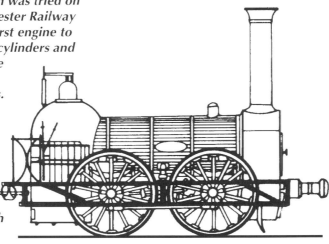

displayed great advantages over what
had gone before. The *Liverpool* had
two axles coupled together, and Bury
used an upright cylinder with a grate
at the bottom and a domed cover to
close the top as a firebox. The boiler
barrel projected out of a flattened
face of the upright cylinder and this
arrangement became known as a
haystack firebox.

Bury used iron bars in place of
plate frames. This feature crossed the
Atlantic and became established in
the USA, as did the haystack firebox
at least for a time. Bar frames were
soon adopted as standard for US
locomotives, and remained so for
many years. Towards the end of the
steam locomotive's life, the whole of
a bar frame for a large locomotive
was poured as a single steel casting,
and this was known as the
locomotive bed.

*This line drawing emphasises Bury's
bar frame, which was to become
more widely deployed in the USA*

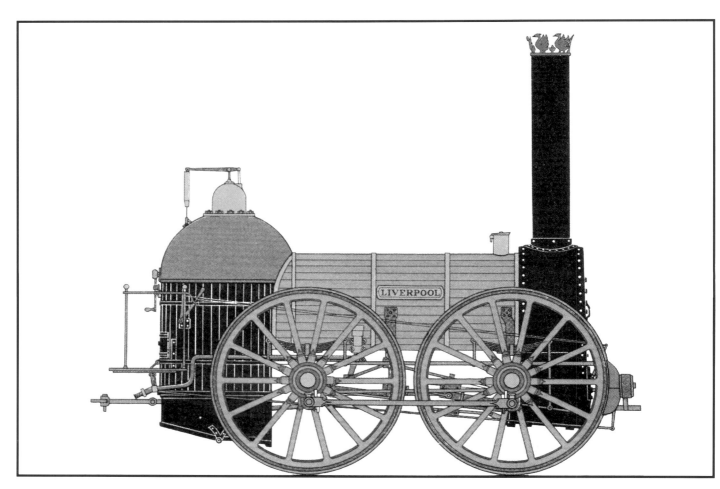

NORTHUMBRIAN 0-2-0

Country of origin: UK
Railway: Liverpool & Manchester Railway (L&M)
Date: 1830
Length overall: 7.315m (24ft)
Total weight: 11,590kg (25,500lb)
Cylinders: two 280 x 406mm (11 x 16in)
Driving wheels: 1.321m (4ft 4in)
Axle load: 2,955kg (6,500lb)
Fuel: 1,000kg (2,200lb) coke
Grate area: 0.75m² (8sq ft)
Water: 1,817 litres (400 Imp gal/480 US gal)

Heating surface: 38m² (412sq ft)
Superheater: none
Steam pressure: 3.5kg/cm² (50psi)
Adhesive weight: 2,955kg (6,500lb)
Tractive force: 720kg (1,580lb)

Bottom: *a drawing based on a contemporary etching of Northumbrian. The locomotive had 132 tubes of 41mm (1.625in) diameter, but its most important development was the internal firebox. It was the first example of a modern locomotive boiler*

Stephenson's *Northumbrian* hauled the opening train of the Liverpool & Manchester Railway in 1830. Unlike the *Rocket* it had a smokebox, in which ashes that had been drawn through the boiler tubes could accumulate, and a boiler that was integrated with the water jacket around the firebox. This combination produced the locomotive-type boiler that was fitted to virtually all of the steam locomotives ever built.

The cylinders of the *Northumbrian* were not only fitted in an accessible position outside of the wheels, but also positioned horizontally. This alleviated the rocking that was inherent in the design of the *Rocket* because the latter's cylinders were steeply inclined, producing out of balance forces.

The *Northumbrian* was built with the use of vertical iron plates as the main frames but suffered through lack of adhesive weight. This made necessary considerable alteration to the *Northumbrian* layout.

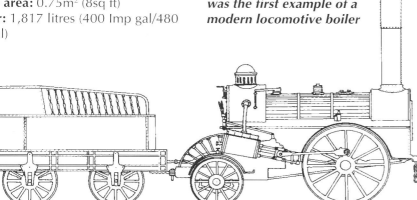

PLANET CLASS 2–2–0

Country of origin: UK
Railway: Liverpool & Manchester Railway (L&M)
Date: 1830
Length overall: 7.42m (24ft 4in)
Total weight: 13,500kg (29,500lb)
Cylinders: two 292 x 406mm (11.5 x 16in)
Driving wheels: 1.57m (5ft 2in)
Axle load: 5,000kg (11,250lb)
Fuel: *ca* 1,000kg (2,200lb) coke
Grate area: 0.67m² (7.2sq ft)
Water: *ca* 1,800 litres (400 Imp gal/480 US gal)
Heating surface: 38m² (407sq ft)

Steam pressure: *ca* 3.5kg/cm² (50psi)
Adhesive weight: 5,000kg (11.250lb)
Tractive force: *ca* 660kg (1,450lb)

Stephenson designed the **Planet** *to have the cylinders placed horizontally and enclosed within the smoke box.* **Planet** *was also the first locomotive to have outside 'sandwich' frames. These frames were normally formed of oak or ash, and strengthened on both sides by iron plates*

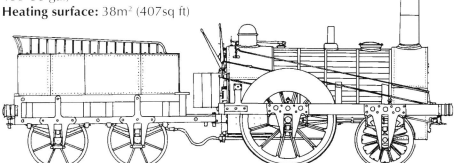

Delivered soon after *Northumbrian*, *Planet* had the cylinders put at the front end, a practice that has since been followed in making virtually all subsequent steam locomotives. This helped both the weight distribution, and the available adhesive weight. The drive was on the rear wheels, which supported the heavy firebox. Furthermore, the cylinders were placed inside rather than outside the wheels, and they were connected to the driving wheels by making the main axle in the form of a double crank. The idea behind this was to cure the 'boxing' motion, which had been a problem featuring in earlier locomotives.

    Planet proved to be reasonably successful, and was the locomotive on which Matthias Baldwin based his own first full-sized locomotive, called *Old Ironsides*, before going on to create the greatest locomotive works in the world. *Planet* was also the locomotive that finally established the Stephensons.

VAUXHALL 2–2–0

Country of origin: Ireland
Railway: Dublin & Kingstown Railway
Date: 1834
(Approximate specification):
Length overall: 7.315m (24ft)
Total weight: not known
Cylinders: two 280 x 457mm (11 x 18in)
Driving wheels: 1.524m (5ft)
Axle load: not known
Fuel: not known
Grate area: not known
Water: not known
Heating surface: not known
Superheater: none
Steam pressure: 3.5kg/cm² (50psi)
Adhesive weight: not known
Tractive force: 700kg (1,550lb)

Below: Forrester & Co's Vauxhall had the advantage of outside horizontal cylinders combined with outside plate frames and bearings

Constructed in 1832 for the Dublin & Kingstown Railway by George Forrester of Liverpool, the *Vauxhall* was the world's first locomotive to have accessible outside cylinders placed horizontally at the front end. It is thus the first example of the final generally-accepted cylinder layout for the early steam locomotives.

Forrester also made improvements to the valve gear, providing a separate eccentric set of valves for both forward and reverse motion on each

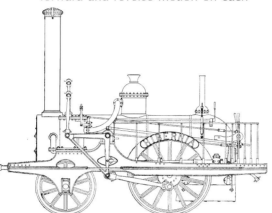

cylinder; that is, four on the driving axle. The reversing lever could move the eccentric rods to engage or disengage the appropriate valve pin by means of V-shaped grabs fitted to the ends of the rods. Although this could only be accomplished while the engine was stationary, it was far easier to engage reverse than when using the slip-eccentric valve gear, which was very difficult to operate from the cab.

The *Vauxhall* achieved a speed of 50km/h (31mph) on its inaugural run; however, these locomotives were not steady, and within a few years all of these Forrester types had been converted to 2–2–2s.

Built at the same time as Vauxhall by Sharp, Roberts & Co, Hibernia, left, had vertical cylinders of 279 x 406mm (11 x 16in), which instead of being sited near the middle of the engine below the platform, were placed just behind the smoke-box and above the leading wheels

DER ADLER 2–2–2

Country of origin: Germany
Railway: Nürnburg-Fürth Railway
Date: 1835
Length overall: 7.62m (25ft)
Total weight: 14,318kg (31,500lb)
engine only
Cylinders: two 229 x 406mm (9 x16in)
Driving wheels: 1.371m (4ft 6in)
Axle load: 6,022kg (13,250lb)
Fuel: not known
Grate area: 0.48m² (5.2sq ft)
Water: not known
Heating surface: 18.2m² (196sq ft)
Steam pressure: 4.2kg/cm² (60psi)
Adhesive weight: 6,022kg (13,250lb)
Tractive force: 550kg (1,220lb)

Although Germany had been building locomotives since 1816, *Der Adler* was the first one to be seen to be successful, when inaugurating the Nürnberg to Fürth railway. After Ludwig I had given his royal assent, this railway later came to be known as the Ludwigsbahn.

The locomotive was a hurried

Stephenson considered that his first short-stroke 2–2–2s for the L & M 'consumed too much water'

Bottom: *the first running of* **Der Adler**

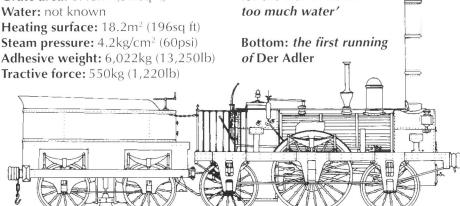

order, placed with the Stephensons after the original contractor had reneged. It is generally thought to have been not too dissimilar to the *Patentee*, which Stephenson had supplied to the Liverpool & Manchester Railway in 1834.

The original Stephenson *Planet* had had inside cylinders and a crank axle. This design he replaced in a 2–2–2 locomotive of 1833 by using driving wheels which had no flanges, and because of its extra axle the loading was reduced. These improvements that he had introduced were registered by Stephenson, hence the name *Patentee*.

Many of the specification details are disputed between various authorities, but it is known that the *Adler* remained in service until 1857, at which point it was sold rather than scrapped. A replica was built in the 1930s, by *Deutsche Reichsbahn* (DR)'s Kaiserslauten works, and this is now in the transport museum at Nürnberg.

NORTH STAR 2–2–2

Country of origin: UK
Railway: Great Western Railway (GWR)
Date: 1837
Length overall: not known
Total weight: 21,100kg (46,420lb) engine only
Cylinders: two 406 x 406mmm (16 x 16in)
Driving wheels: 2.45m (8ft)
Axle load: not known
Fuel: not known
Grate area: 1.25m² (13.5sq ft)
Water: not known
Heating surface: 66.05m² (711sq ft)
Superheater: none
Steam pressure: 4.2kg/cm² (60psi)
Adhesive weight: 9,800kg (21,560lb)
Tractive force: 822kg (1,810lb)

Charles Collett's reconstructed drawing of North Star, 1925

Below: the North Star replica, photographed at Swindon in 1957

Daniel Gooch was trained at Charles Tayleur's works at Newton-le-Willows in Lancashire, and was appointed superintendent to the Great Western Railway (GWR) in 1837. On his appointment, he discovered that the locomotives then being employed were quite inadequate to haul the trains. They had been built to a Brunel specification, with wheels that

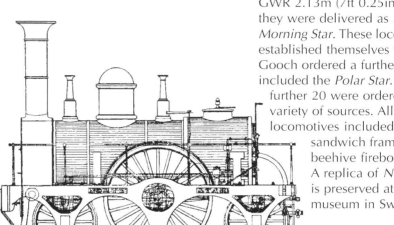

were excessively large and cylinder sizes that were too small to give the output required.

Gooch then discovered that Robert Stephenson & Co had two engines built for the 1.67m (5ft 6in) gauge, awaiting payment before being shipped to the New Orleans Railroad. Gooch persuaded Stephenson's to rebuild them for the GWR 2.13m (7ft 0.25in) gauge, and they were delivered as *North Star* and *Morning Star*. These locomotives established themselves well, and Gooch ordered a further ten which included the *Polar Star*. Later on a further 20 were ordered from a variety of sources. All of these locomotives included sandwich frames and beehive fireboxes. A replica of *North Star* is preserved at the GWR museum in Swindon.

BURY TYPE 2–2–0

Country of origin: UK
Railway: London & Birmingham Railway (L&B)
Date: 1837
Length overall: 8.17m (26ft 9.5ir)
Total weight: 10,000kg (22,000lb)
Cylinders: two 280 x 415mm (11 x 16.5in)
Driving wheels: 1.55m (5ft 0.75in)
Axle load: 5,700kg (12,600lb)
Grate area: 0.65m² (7sq ft)
Heating surface: 33.2m² (357sq ft)
Steam pressure: 3.5kg/cm² (50psi)
Adhesive weight: 5,700kg (12,600lb)
Tractive force: 629kg (1,386lb)

Edward Bury built no less than 58 locomotives with this 2–2–2 wheel arrangement for passenger work on the London & Birmingham Railway. The Railway was inaugurated in 1837 by these small, underpowered locomotives, the last of which was delivered in 1841. Even by the time

Edward Bury, 1794-1858, was in charge of the motive power of the London & Birmingham Railway; bottom, a Bury 2–2–0 on the London to Birmingham railway, 1845

that these deliveries had begun, this railway was already the most important in the UK.

Bury had a small locomotive works in Liverpool, and he had initially intended to compete in the Rainhill Trials, but was not ready in time with his entrant, *Liverpool*. This was eventually delivered to the Liverpool & Manchester Railway.

The outer firebox of his 1837 locomotives was circular in plan, with a domed top attached to a normal cylindrical barrel by a circumferential joint. The inner firebox was D-shaped, with the flat side facing towards the front. The problem with this circular shape, however, was that the length could not be greater than the width, since the width was also limited by having to be positioned between the wheels; thus the size of the fire to power output was strictly limited. One saving grace of the *Bury* was that it was cheap to build, and reliable when in service.

LION 0–4–2

Country of origin: UK

Railway: Liverpool & Manchester Railway (L&M)

Date: 1838

Length overall: 10.287m (33ft 9in)

Total weight: 19,200kg (42,300lb)

Cylinders: two 305 x 457mm (12 x 18in)

Driving wheels: 1.524m (5ft)

Axle load: not known

Fuel: not known

Grate area: 1.04m² (11.2sq ft)

Water: not known

Heating surface: 46.5m² (500sq ft)

Superheater: none

Steam pressure: 3.5kg/cm² (50psi)

Adhesive weight: not known

Tractive force: 833kg (1,836lb)

Lion was originally built by Todd Kitson & Laird to haul coal trains. Its replica took a starring role in the film **The Tichfield Thunderbolt**

This locomotive has many claims to fame. It was built by Todd, Kitson and Laird of Leeds, at a time when the basic format of steam locomotives was becoming established and specialisation of locomotives for specific tasks was also becoming the norm. *Lion* was sold to the Mersey Docks and Harbour Board for use as a shunting engine in 1859. Years later, it was set up as a stationary engine, a duty it performed until 1920, when the London, Midland & Scottish (LMS) railway purchased the remains. It was then restored as a locomotive and run at the centenary celebrations of the Liverpool & Manchester Railway, is now preserved at the Merseyside County Museum, Liverpool, and today is the world's oldest working locomotive.

The *Lion* has a square-section firebox, known as a haycock. This is crowned by a domed roof and sandwich frames enclose the wheels. *Lion* was designed to have a top speed of 72km/h (45mph), and to pull freight trains of up to 208 tonnes (200 tons).

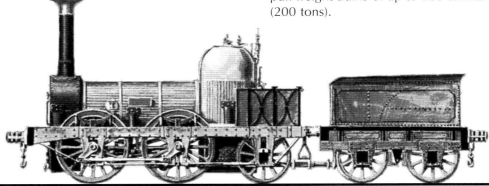

FIRE FLY CLASS 2–2–2

Country of origin: UK
Railway: Great Western Railway (GWR)
Date: 1840
Length overall: 12m (39ft 4in)
Total weight: 42,045kg (92,500lb)
Cylinders: two 381 x 457mm (15 x 18in)
Driving wheels: 2.134m (7ft)
Axle load: 11,363kg (25,000lb)
Fuel: 1,545kg (3,400lb) coke
Grate area: 1.25m² (13.5sq ft)
Water: 8,280 litres (1,800 Imp gal/ 2,160 US gal)
Heating surface: 65m² (700sq ft)
Superheater: none
Steam pressure: 3.5kg/cm² (50psi)
Adhesive weight: 11,363kg (25,000lb)
Tractive force: 929kg (2,049lb)

Right: Centaur was built by Nasmyth, Gaskell & Co in 1841, and was similar to the Fire Fly class

When Isambard Kingdom Brunel was made engineer of the Great Western Railway (GWR) in 1833, he chose a gauge for the railway of 2.14m (7ft 0.25in). This was the widest gauge ever to be used for a railway, and was considerably larger than that standardised for convenience by the Stephensons.

Initially the GWR ordered a variety of locomotives from a variety of builders. None of these was really successful, largely because of the arbitrary restrictions that Brunel imposed upon them which artificially limited their capabilities; for example, six-wheeled locomotives could not exceed 10.7 tonnes (10.5 tons), nor could their piston speed exceed 85m (280ft) per minute. Thus for a long time the GWR made do with a single Patentee-type locomotive, *North Star*, which itself fell far short of Brunel's stipulations.

Brunel then employed Daniel Gooch, who drew up plans based on Stephenson's Patentees, for 62 express train locomotives. The first of these was *Fire Fly*, which was built by Jones, Turner and Evans.

Gooch also ordered a further 38 locomotives for freight work. These were 2–4–0s and 0–6–0s, with boilers, tenders, motion and many other parts common to all the types.

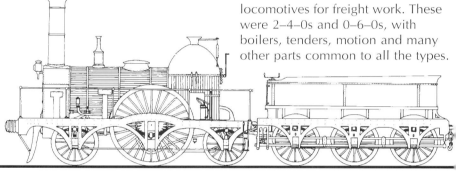

BEUTH 2–2–2

Country of origin: Germany
Railway: Berlin-Anhalt Railway
Date: 1843
Length overall: 6.14m (20ft 2in) engine only
Total weight: 18,500kg (41,000lb) engine only
Cylinders: two 330 x 560mm (13.1 x 22.3in)
Driving wheels: 1.54m (5ft 0.75in)
Axle load: 9,500kg (20,000lb)
Fuel: 1,545kg (3,400lb) coke
Grate area: 0.83m² (8.9sq ft)
Water: 8,280 litres (1,800 Imp gal/ 2,160 US gal)
Heating surface: 47m² (500sq ft)
Steam pressure: 5.5kg/cm² (78psi)
Adhesive weight: 9,500kg (20,000lb)
Tractive force: 1,870kg (4,120lb)

Three German manufacturers, Borsig of Berlin, Maffie of München and Emil Kessler of Karlsruhe, all supplied their first steam locomotives in 1841. Borsig's first engines were a series of 15, all based on William Norris' 4–2–0s which were being imported into Germany at the time. Borsig's locomotives had bar frames and large haycock fireboxes, but they also incorporated a few improvements of their own. They were to prove very successful, and there followed on from them a series of 2–2–2 locomotives, of which *Beuth* was one.

Equal spacing of the axles provided excellent weight distribution. Flat side valves above the cylinders were driven by Stephenson's new link motion, with an auxiliary slide valve to control expansion. Borsig also fitted cylinder drain cocks, which could be operated from the footplate far more easily than those on Norris' engine, which were operated by levers on the cylinders themselves.

The boiler feed pumps were driven by levers attached to the crank pin, and extended back to a position under the cab.

The firebox was elliptical in horizontal section, and the upper part formed a large steam space. There was a cylindrical casing on top of the firebox, which housed the steam pipe and a Salter type of safety valve.

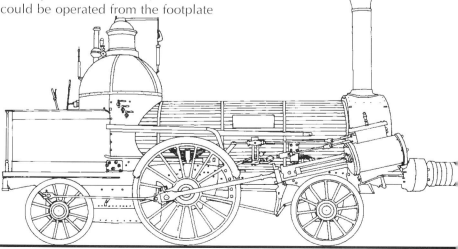

BUDDICOM CLASS 2–2–2

Country of origin: France
Railway: Paris-Rouen Railway
Date: 1843
Length overall: 6.48m (21ft 3.12in) engine only
Total weight: 12,900kg (28,380lb)
Cylinders: two 318 x 533mm (12.2 x 21in)
Driving wheels: 1.72m (5ft 7.7in)
Axle load: 6,600kg (14,550lb)
Fuel: 1,850kg (4,070lb)
Grate area: 0.9m² (9.9sq ft)
Water: 3,600 litres (792 Imp gal/945 US gal)
Heating surface: 48.5m² (534sq ft)
Steam pressure: 5kg/cm² (70psi)
Adhesive weight: 6,300kg (13,860lb)
Tractive force: 1,460kg (3,100lb)

The Crewe type of outside-cylinder locomotive was an important landmark in locomotive history, and had an effect on locomotive design for the next 40 years, influencing French practice especially

William Barbour Buddicom introduced the Crewe type to France, designing locomotives known to the French in his honour as Buddicoms. In those early days of railway development, England had a great impact on French locomotives and rolling stock; even the railwaymen came from England. Left-handed running in France, and the 1.435m (4ft 8.5in) track gauge adopted, are clear signs of this early influence. Furthermore, in 1843 the Paris-Rouen Railway established an Anglo-French company which had mainly British shareholders.

A Buddicom had two outside cylinders that were inclined, a stout double frame, a deep firebox placed between the second and third axles and they had also Stephenson's new link motion fitted.

St Pierre was built at Rouen in 1844, and is now on exhibition at the *Musée Français du Chemin de Fer* (French Railway Museum), Mulhouse. It is the oldest original locomotive on display on the European mainland; it is not a replica but the genuine article, and furthermore it is in running condition. It was one of a class of 40 locomotives used to haul passenger trains between Paris and Rouen.

L'AIGLE 2–2–24

Country of origin: France
Railway: Avignon to Marseilles
Date: 1846
Length overall: 6.97m (22ft 10in)
engine only
Total weight: 22,100kg (48,730lb)
Cylinders: two 330 x 610mm (13.1 x 24in)
Driving wheels: 1.7m (5ft 7in)
Grate area: 0.83m² (8.9sq ft)
Heating surface: 58m² (624sq ft)
Steam pressure: 6kg/cm² (85.3psi)
Adhesive weight: 10,100kg (22,270lb)

Initially, rolling stock was imported into France from England, or was built in France from English drawings. Alfred Hallette of Arras was one of the first French railway engine builders, and built the *Sezanne* locomotive to British specifications. It was a long-boiler Stephenson type, and entered service with the Troyes-based Montereau company in 1847.

It was one of 16 locomotives to be ordered by the company, which merged with the Paris, Lyons & Méditerranée (PLM) in 1853, after which the locomotives ran on the line from Paris to Strasbourg.

L'Aigle belonged to the same generation of Stephenson long-boiler locomotives, but was built in 1846 in the Stephenson works in Newcastle and was bought for the line from Avignon to Marseilles. Delivery of the locomotive was effected by sea.

These two locomotives are strikingly different in appearance, the British version having wood, copper and brass fittings, while the French one by contrast is much simpler, though technically similar. Both were saved from the scrapyard by sheer good fortune; one was being used as a steam generator at Ollins, the other for 50 years had been a standby transportable steam locomotive. Both are now restored, at Mulhouse.

Below and bottom:
L'Aigle *was built for the Avignon to Marseilles railway in 1846*

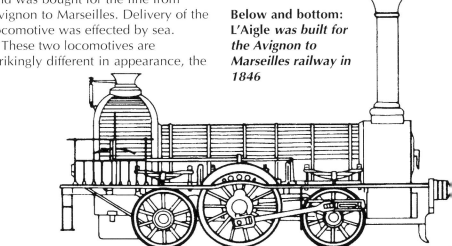

CRAMPTON TYPE 4–2–0

Country of origin: France
Railway: Est (Eastern) railway
Date: 1852
Length overall: 12.728m (41ft 9in)
Total weight: 47,727kg (105,000lb)
Cylinders: two 400 x 500mm (15.75 x 21.5in)
Driving wheels: 2.1m (6ft 10.75in)
Axle load: 12,500kg (27,500lb)
Fuel: 7,045kg (15,500lb)
Grate area: 1.42m² (15.3sq ft)
Water: 7,084 litres (1,540 Imp gal/ 1,850 US gal)
Heating surface: 98.4m² (1,059sq ft)
Steam pressure: 6.5kg/cm² (92psi)
Adhesive weight: 12,318kg (27,100lb)
Tractive force: 2,290kg (5,040lb)

The Crampton engine Namur, right, was built for the Namur-Liège railway in 1846 by Tulk & Ley; Le Continent, below, was built for the Paris to Strasbourg railway, which later became the Est (Eastern) railway, in 1852

Crampton had worked under Gooch at the Great Western Railway, and while there applied to patent a high-speed locomotive with a low centre of gravity. In order to achieve the latter, Crampton placed the driving axle behind the boiler with the cylinders outside the wheels and well back from the front of the engine.

On obtaining his patent, Crampton set up in business. His first engine, *Namur*, was a 4–2–0 built for the Belgian Namur-Liège railway

although trials were first conducted in the UK. A total of 320 Cramptons were built with the majority going to French railways, so great an influence that for some time his name entered the French language to mean 'train'.

At one time a Crampton held the world speed record, when No 604 was run at 144km/h (89.5mph) with a load of 159.5 tonnes (157 tons), on 20 June 1890. At the time it was undergoing trials for the Paris, Lyons & Méditerranée (PLM) railway.

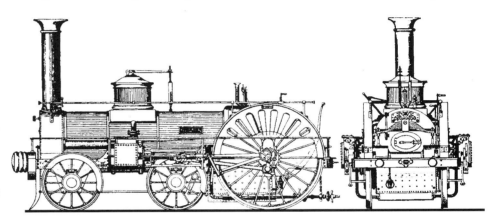

American Locomotive Development 1830–1855

Best Friend of Charleston 0–4–0T

Country of origin: USA
Railway: South Carolina Railroad (SCRR)
Date: 1830
Length overall: 4.5m (14ft 9in)
Total weight: 4,081kg (9,000lb)
Cylinders: two 152 x 406mm (6 x 16in)
Driving wheels: 1.37m (4ft 6in)
Axle load: 2,000kg (4,500lb)
Water: 640 litres (140 Imp gal/165 US gal)
Steam pressure: 3.5kg/cm² (50psi)
Adhesive weight: 4,081kg (9,000lb)
Tractive force: 206kg (453lb)

The first full-sized steam locomotive to be built in the United States entered service on 15 January 1831 on America's first commercial railway, the South Carolina Railroad. Then also the longest railway in the world, it ran from Charleston to Hamburg, a distance of some 248km (154 miles).

The *Best Friend of Charleston* was constructed at the West Point Foundry in New York, and was unusual in that it featured a vertical boiler. It also had a well tank integral with the locomotive, four coupled wheels and two gently-inclined cylinders.

The locomotive proved quite successful, being able to handle a train of five cars each with ten passengers, at a speed of 32km/h (20mph). Later versions of the type had horizontal boilers, however.

A boiler explosion later in that same year, 1831, was thought to have been caused by the fireman having tied down the safety valve lever. As a result, legislation was promulgated which introduced tamper-proof valves.

A reconstruction of the first steam locomotive to be placed in regular service in the United States

JOHN BULL 0–4–0

Country of origin: USA
Railway: Camden & Amboy Railroad
Date: 1831
Length overall: 11.28m (37ft)
Total weight: 10,500kg (23,100lb)
Cylinders: two 228 x 508mm (9 x 20in)
Driving wheels: 1.37m (4ft 6in)
Axle load: not known
Fuel: not known
Grate area: 0.9m² (10sq ft)
Water: not known
Heating surface: 28m² (300sq ft)
Superheater: none
Steam pressure: 2.1kg/cm² (30psi)
Adhesive weight: 10,500kg (23,100lb)
Tractive force: 347kg (765lb)

Robert Stephenson & Co built the *John Bull* in England, and delivered it to the Camden and Amboy Railroad on 31 August 1831. The locomotive was placed in regular service at Bordentown, New Jersey, later that year and was the first locomotive to run on what was to become the Pennsylvania Railroad system.

Unfortunately, *John Bull*'s weight at 10.46 tonnes (10.3 tons) was too much for the track, and it was withdrawn; fortunately, it is now preserved, at the Smithsonian Institution in Washington DC.

This locomotive was followed by a number of so-called grasshopper engines, built by Ross Winans for the Baltimore & Ohio Railroad between 1832 and 1837. After that time, the 0–4–0 type ceased to be an operational tool for the increasing demands of the American railroads of the day.

John Bull *started work on 12 November 1831 and was withdrawn in 1866. A wedge-shaped cowcatcher was mounted at the front of the timber frame, for the first time*

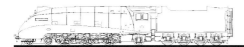

LAFAYETTE 4–2–0

Country of origin: USA
Railway: Baltimore & Ohio Railroad (B&O)
Date: 1837
Length overall: 9.25m (30ft 4.25in)
Total weight: 20,000kg (44,000lb)
Cylinders: 268 x 457mm (10.5 x 18in)
Driving wheels: 1.22m (4ft)
Axle load: 6,000kg (13,000lb)
Fuel: 1,000kg (2,200lb) coke
Grate area: 0.8m² (8.6sq ft)
Water: 2,070 litres (450 Imp gal/540 US gal)
Heating surface: 36.6m² (394sq ft)
Superheater: none
Steam pressure: 4.2kg/cm² (60psi)
Adhesive weight: 13,500kg (30,000lb)
Tractive force: 957kg (2,162lb)

A typical 4–2–0 type, built by William Norris

The *Lafayette* was a typical William Norris 4–2–0 construction, but it was the first to combine inclined outside cylinders, a large domed firebox, a short-wheelbase leading bogie and bar frames. Moreover, it was the first locomotive with a horizontal boiler to be employed by the Baltimore & Ohio Railroad when it entered service in 1837.

The B&O had been the first public railroad to be granted a charter in the USA for both freight and passenger transport. Initially it opened a 19.3km (12-mile) stretch of line in 1930, but the carriages were horse-drawn and steam did not take over until 1834, when grasshopper type locomotives displaced horsepower.

The Lafayette series of locomotives ran to a class of eight, all of which proved to be very successful and reasonably reliable. Norris went on to become the first US exporter of steam locomotives when, also in 1837, he sold a similar locomotive to the Vienna-Raab railway.

Norris continued to export locomotives to Austria, Canada, Germany and even the UK until 1842, and some of these remained in service until 1856. The company went on to become the largest locomotive builder in the USA for a short time, supplying 4–4–0s, 0–6–0s and 4–6–0s in addition to the 4–2–0s. However, other manufacturers copied Norris' designs, and the company never received its just deserts.

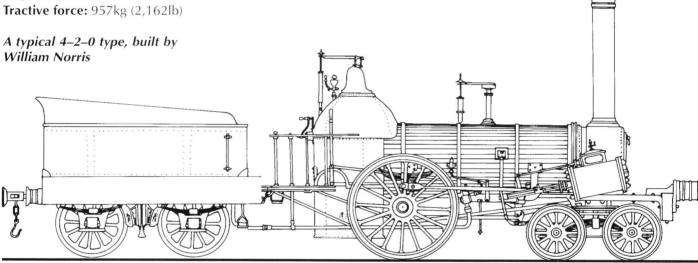

MUD-DIGGER 0–8–0

Country of origin: USA
Railway: Baltimore & Ohio Railroad (B&O)
Date: 1844
Length overall: 6.05m (19ft 10in) engine only
Total weight: 21,363kg (47,000lb) engine only
Cylinders: two 432 x 610mm (17 x 24in)
Driving wheels: 0.84m (2ft 9in)
Axle load: 5,875kg (12,925lb)
Fuel: not known
Grate area: not known
Water: not known
Heating surface: not known
Superheater: none
Steam pressure: not known
Adhesive weight: 21,363kg (47,000lb)
Tractive force: not known

Ross Winans became the locomotive engineer on the Baltimore & Ohio Railroad (B&O) at the Mount Clare shops, where he was employed for 25 years. He designed the first eight-wheeled passenger car in the world, and is also credited with introducing the mounting of the car on two bogies.

Winans built the first locomotive to be exported from the USA in 1837, and in 1841 he built the first 0–8–0 locomotive, for the B&O. He introduced the first of the vertical-boiler *Mud-Digger* 0–8–0s in 1837, which in 1848 were followed by the 0–8–0 wide-firebox Camel type. These were designed to burn anthracite, and he built over 100 of them for the B&O; they were the first 0–8–0s to be produced in any quantity. They also featured the positioning of the driver's cab on top of the boiler.

The Baldwin locomotive company was also an early producer of the 0–8–0 type, building about 150 of them for the Pennsylvania & Reading Railroad.

JOHN STEVENS 6–2–0

Country of origin: USA
Railway: Camden & Amboy Railroad
Date: 1849
Length overall: 9.04m (29ft 8in)
engine only
Total weight: 22,727kg (50,000lb)
engine only
Cylinders: two 330 x 863mm (13 x 34in)
Driving wheels: not known
Axle load: not known
Fuel: not known
Grate area: 1.82m² (19.82sq ft)
Water: not known
Heating surface: not known
Superheater: none
Steam pressure: not known
Adhesive weight: not known
Tractive force: not known

Colonel John Stevens built a screw-propelled steam boat in 1802, and his first steam wagon in 1824, shown here being demonstrated in front of his house

Colonel John Stevens is considered to be the father of American railroads. He experimented with railway building for some years, and in October 1824 he demonstrated a small circular line on his own farm in Hoboken, New Jersey.

On this line, fitted for rack rail propulsion, he ran a small steam locomotive which had a vertical boiler. Although this never ran outside the confines of Stevens' farm, it aroused great interest and gave a strong impetus to the building of America's first true railroads.

Colonel Stevens designed a Crampton-type locomotive in 1848, of which eight were built by William Norris. These had large driving wheels, and three-axle bogies to carry the boiler barrels. The cylinders were very long, and mounted outside the frame with complicated valve gear. The boiler fire door was under the driving wheel axle with a correspondingly low platform for the fireman, while the driver's cab was

high up above the boiler.

Stevens had obtained a State charter to build and operate a steam railroad between New Brunswick and Trenton, New Jersey, but this charter expired without the railroad having been built. However, the idea persisted and on 7 March 1823 the New Jersey Railroad & Transport Company (NJRR&TC) was chartered to build across the State. It was not until 1 January 1839 that the railroad was finally opened, between New Brunswick and Trenton. The NJRR&TC itself was later to become part of the Pennsylvania Railroad.

Two sons, Robert and Edwin, shared the Colonel's interest, and were able to build the famous Camden & Amboy Railroad under a charter which they were granted in 1830. They developed a virtual monopoly for the journey between New York city and Philadelphia, which was made initially in seven hours at a fare of $3.00.

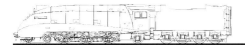

STEAM'S GOLDEN YEARS

British express services were easily the fastest in the world during the 1880s, though trains were relatively light and sustained speeds of 64.4 to 80.5km/h (40 to 50mph) were usual rather than really high maximum speeds. The introduction of the bogie passenger carriages during the 1870s enabled a new level of comfort to be provided and, together with the adoption of continuous brakes, block signalling and other safety measures, permitted considerably higher speeds. Improved track also encouraged faster running, and towards the end of the 1880s scheduled services were already becoming faster.

The premier long-distance journey was that from London to Edinburgh. The east-coast lines pushed the speed to an average of 97.6km/h (60.6mph) on 21 August 1889, using one of the Great Northern's Stirling 2.438m (8ft) singles between King's Cross and York and North Eastern and North British 4–4–0s for the remainder of the journey. On the following night, the west-coast companies replied with a time of 8 hours 32 minutes for the 869.4km (540-mile) trip for a record average speed of 101.8km/h (63mph). The engines involved in this achievement were a three-cylinder compound 4–4–0 run between Euston and Crewe and the Precedent class 2–4–0 *Hardwicke* from Crewe to Carlisle, these being followed by Caledonian Railway 4–4–0s for the rest of the run to Aberdeen.

Meanwhile, the development of railways in the United States had followed a radically different course from that in Britain. Despite some early setbacks they continued to spread, and by 1850 there were some 14,490km (9,000 miles) of railway in operation. Another decade saw that total more than trebled, but the 1860s brought the

Civil War and a temporary pause in new construction.

By the time the War ended in 1865, the United States Military Railroads (USMRR) was operating more than 400 locomotives and 6,000 cars, controlled over 3,220km (2,000 miles) of track, and had been responsible for the repair of many bridges and sections of track that had been destroyed by enemy action.

The most significant single wartime development, however, was the formal chartering of the first transcontinental railway. President Lincoln had signed the Act in July 1862, authorising the

construction of the Pacific railroad. This was to be built between the banks of the Missouri (at the site which became the city of Omaha, Nebraska), and Sacramento, California. The final joining of the two sets of track was made at Promontory, Utah, on 10 May 1869. Golden spikes were driven to join the actual rails, and representative locomotives from each of the railroads steamed forward to touch pilots in a symbolic meeting of east and west.

The completion of the first trans-continental line marked the start of a period of unparalleled expansion of the American rail network. Further new transcontinental lines were built as the Southern Pacific and Santa Fe railroads crossed the southern territories, and the

*Central Pacific's **Jupiter** is on the left and Union Pacific's **No 119** to the right at Promontory, Utah, on 10 May 1869. With the spike driven, Chief Engineers General Grenville Dodge of Union and Samuel Montague of Central shake hands*

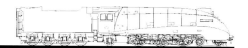

A Currier & Ives print of 1868, depicting the opening up of the west by the railroads

Northern Pacific, Great Northern, Burlington and Milwaukee railroads spanned the northwest. Connecting lines were built in all directions, and by the end of the century there was a network of 310,730km (193,000 miles) of railroad.

In Britain, daily services were run between London and Birmingham at 89.4km/h (55.5mph) by 1902, and in 1903 the fastest service on the run to Bristol was scheduled at just under 96.6km/h (60mph). In 1904 the *City of Truro* inaugurated the *Cornish Riviera* express, the longest non-stop run in the world, which averaged 89.4km/h 55.5mph) for the 395.3km (245.5-mile) journey.

The growing weight of these fast services called for more powerful locomotives, and the logical step was to add a third pair of driving wheels. This solution was adopted by most of the main-line companies before the First World War, most successfully on the Great Western in the form of the series of 4–6–0s designed by George Churchward. His two-cylinder Saint and four-cylinder Star classes were outstanding engines, and after his retirement in 1921 the Star type was developed into the famous Castle class.

The first of the Castles, *Caerphilly Castle*, appeared in 1923, and the type proved so successful that modified versions were still being built in 1950. The four-cylinder 4–6–0s of the Lord Nelson class, which were provided to deal with the heaviest expresses on the Southern Railway, were designed after studies of the Castle class.

Churchward's influence also led to the Stanier-designed Black Five 4–6–0s, of which no fewer than 842 were built between 1934 and 1951, and which proved capable of virtually any type of work.

Meanwhile the trend in the biggest passenger engines had been towards the Pacific type, on which the pair of rear carrying wheels allowed a bigger firebox to be used.

Production of the A3 Pacifics began in 1928, and the new engines were spectacularly successful. In March 1935, on a special train run between the King's Cross terminal in London and Newcastle-upon-Tyne, the A3 *Papyrus* covered well over half of the 864.6km (537-mile) round trip at 128.8km/h (80mph), reaching a maximum speed of 173.9km/h (108mph) and recording an average of 112.3km/h (69.8mph) for the return trip from Newcastle. The first of the A3 Pacific designs, *Silver Link*, made its public début on a special trial in September 1935, breaking more records with a top speed of 181.1km/h (112.5mph).

In 1933, the London, Midland & Scottish Railway (LMS) introduced the new Princess Royal class Pacifics for its *Royal Scot* service between London and Glasgow. Following the introduction of the streamlined *Silver Jubilee* train, the company set about producing its own streamlined Pacifics. The first of the new

Above: *Castle class No 5086 Viscount Horne passes Reading West in 1954*

"THE SILVER JUBILEE"

BRITAIN'S FIRST STREAMLINE TRAIN

NEWCASTLE AND LONDON IN 4 HOURS

AVERAGE THROUGHOUT SPEED 67.08 M.P.H.

Weekdays (Saturdays excepted) from 30th September 1935

NEWCASTLE dep 10.0 | KING'S CROSS dep 5.30
DARLINGTON " 10.42 | DARLINGTON " 8.48
KING'S CROSS arr. 2.0 | NEWCASTLE arr. 9.30

Connecting trains serve Tyneside and Teesside

SUPPLEMENTARY FARES First Class 5/- Third Class 3/-

LONDON & NORTH EASTERN RAILWAY

Right: *a poster announcing the Silver Jubilee, Britain's first streamlined train*

Above right: *Mallard prepares to leave Grantham station with an up Leeds and Bradford express*

Right: *King Arthur class No 777 at Eastleigh works*

engines was built for the *Coronatio[n] Scot* service which was inaugurated i[n] 1937, and was scheduled to cover th[e] 645.6km (401 miles) between Londo[n] and Glasgow in an impressive six an[d] a half hours.

By this time, the London & Nort[h] Eastern Railway (LNER) had introduce[d] a six-hour service between London an[d] Edinburgh named the *Coronation*. Thi[s] made necessary speeds of 161km/[h] (100mph) on many stretches, and i[n] 1938 the company made an all-ou[t] attempt at a new speed record whil[e] ostensibly carrying out braking trials[.] The engine was the A4 Pacific *Mallar[d]* which on 3 July reached a speed o[f] 202.9km/h (126mph) with the *Silve[r] Jubilee* train fitted with a specia[l] dynamometer car which recorded th[e] performance. The record was estab[-] lished only at the cost of sever[e] overheating, and the following year th[e] intervention of the Second World Wa[r] put a stop to further attempts a[t] increased speeds on the Scottis[h] services.

Oliver Bulleid became the chief mechanical engineer for the Southern Railway in 1937, which had for some years already been busily engaged in electrifying sections of its main line. Bulleid's first move was to improve many examples of the existing Lord Nelson, King Arthur and Schools classes by the addition of Lemaître multiple blast pipes. Bulleid's original designs showed a marked tendency to innovation on a comprehensive scale. The most readily obvious feature of his Merchant Navy class Pacifics. which first appeared in 1941, was the 'air-smoothed' casing, but along with the striking exterior came a wealth of novel details. The valve gear was enclosed in an oil bath; the firebox and high-pressure boiler, which were tapered underneath to accommodate the inside cylinder, were of welded steel; the wheels were an adaption of the north American Boxpok type, and minor features included electric lighting and steam-powered fire doors.

Above: *Schools class No 30915* **Brighton** *prepared for the Derby Da Royal Train, June 1953*

Below: *Merchant Navy class No 35017* **Belgian Marine** *under trial*

State ownership of railways began much earlier on the European mainland than in Britain. Alongside the principal companies in France such as the Nord, st, Midi, Ouest, Paris-Orléans (PO) and the Paris, Lyons & Méditerranée (PLM) which had been organised to adiate from Paris, the État or state ystem was formed from a group of the mall companies in the west of the country in 1878.

The result was to create a competitor or the PO on the route to Bordeaux, while the Midi's control of the routes to Spain meant that the PO's services ied with those of the other connecting ine, the PLM. With this stimulus, the PO built up a fleet of the fastest trains n the country in the late nineteenth entury. It introduced the first engines of the Pacific type to Europe in 1907, or its difficult main line to Toulouse.

These were four-cylinder de Glehn ompounds, and a second series with uperheaters was followed by a third vith even bigger driving wheels for the igher speed services on the Bordeaux

line. The compound system developed by Alfred de Glehn and Gaston du Bousquet used a pair of high-pressure cylinders outside to drive the second pair of coupled wheels and a low-pressure pair inside, acting on the leading axle. The system was used widely in France and elsewhere in Europe.

Among the most prestigious of the French services was the Nord boat train that formed the connection between Paris and Calais or Boulogne. Gaston du Bousquet's death in 1910 had put an end to the development of the 4–8–4 design for the Nord that he had been working on, and the company was

forced to adopt 4–6–2s (Pacifics) of a type that had already been developed by de Glehn for the Alsace-Lorraine railway.

Below: *the British locomotive builder Sharp, Roberts & Co built 2–4–0s for the PLM and Nord (Northern) railways of France in 1867. The mixed-traffic engines for the latter railway had 1.8m (5ft 10.5in) driving wheels, and worked fish trains from the Channel ports to Paris*

Bottom: *an SNCF Class 231 K4 at Pont-de-Briques, with the up Flèche d'Or*

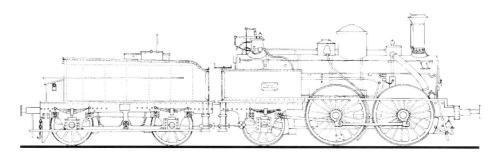

After the First World War, the Nord planned a new class of super Pacifics using the larger steam passages already developed for the 4–6–0. The first example had been designed by George Asselin in 1914, incorporating the relatively small wheels and enlarged steam passages to give the necessary higher piston speeds earlier proposed by du Bousquet for a 4–6–0. Production had been delayed by the First World War, but after their introduction in 1923 these locomotives proved to be capable of extremely heavy work. The last batch, the Collin super Pacifics introduced in 1931, were able to maintain 96.6km/h (60mph) schedules with the 508-tonne (500-ton) boat trains between Paris and the Channel ports.

While these engines were being built for the Nord, one of the greatest of all locomotive designers had started work in the research department of the Paris-Orléans company. This was André Chapelon, who concentrated his efforts on improving the circulation of the steam. To this end he introduced internal streamlining of the steam passages. He was also able to increase the temperature in the superheaters to enable superheated steam to be fed to the low pressure cylinders. At the same time he adapted a device originated by the Finnish engineer Kylala for dividing the steam jet from the blast pipe to give improved draught on the fire without restricting the flow of the exhaust steam from the cylinders.

The result of these improvements, when applied to a PO Pacific, was an increase in power of 50%, along with more economical use of fuel. Once the details became known, other French railways bought either new or rebuilt PO locomotives that were being made redundant by electrification, or applied Chapelon's principles to their own designs. By 1938, when the various companies were absorbed into the *Société National des Chemins de Fer* (SNCF, the French national railway company), Chapelon's influence was already dominant although it was some years before he succeeded to the office of chief engineer.

Both State-owned and the private railways had been built from the beginning in Germany, and thus the formation of the German railway federation in 1917 was followed by the gradual absorption of the private lines into the State system. The dominant member of the federation was Prussia, and after the First World War the majority of the locomotives built for the new *Deutsche Reichsbahn* (State railway) were Prussian types.

However, the south German states of Bavaria, Baden and Württemberg had produced many distinctive designs, and the Bavarian railway had pioneered the use of 4–6–0 and Pacific types for express passenger trains. The Bavarian S3/6 class Pacific, introduced in 1908, was the only non-Prussian type to be built for the Reichsbahn. They were constructed by the firm of Maffei, and

were used on the fastest German trains which included the famous *Rheingold* express along the Rhine valley.

Of course, the important German contribution to steam locomotive design was the superheating system developed by Wilhelm Schmidt in the late 1880s. The purpose of superheating was to raise the temperature of the steam well above that produced in the boiler so that after expanding in the cylinders it would still be hot enough to avoid the condensation that occurred otherwise.

Various attempts were made to achieve the necessary extra degree of heating, but it was Schmidt's fire tube system that superseded all others. Steam from the boiler was collected in a header in the smokebox, then led through enlarged fire tubes by narrow pipes, which doubled back to a second compartment in the header, whence it was fed to the cylinders.

The Prussian State railway was among the first to adopt the new device, which enabled it to dispense with compound operation. Another benefit was that the superheated steam was able to do more work than the ordinary saturated steam so that boiler pressures could be reduced and larger cylinders used instead. This resulted in lower running costs and a considerable reduction in maintenance requirements.

A typical 4–4–0, built for the Prussian State Railway in 1893

The most famous Prussian locomotive of this period was the Class
P8 4–6–0. Some 3,850 of these were
built, 3,370 going to the State railway
alone. They remained in service for
many years, and after the First World
War they were used by several other
countries which received them as part
of the war reparations Germany was
obliged to make after the Armistice.

Richard Wagner was responsible for
the introduction of new locomotive
designs for the Reichsbahn in the
period between the two world wars.
Among his products was the Class 01
Pacific, which, along with the later 03,
became a standard type. The principal
passenger express locomotives of the
period were the 231 examples of his
01 series, despite their typically low
pressures and two-cylinder simple
machinery which meant that they were
not the fastest of engines. This was
counterbalanced by their durability.

After the Second World War, both the
name and many of the locomotives of
the Deutsche Reichsbahn were taken

over by the German Democratic
Republic, and a number of 01s were
rebuilt with bigger boilers, Boxpok
wheels, Giesl ejectors and other
modifications.

**Above: a Deutsche Reichsbahn
Class 03 locomotive at Magdeburg in
1976; the prototype Class 05
streamlined 4–6–4, No 05.001, below**

Another of Wagner's designs was the
streamlined Class 05 4–6–4, but it was
destined to remain at the prototype
stage. The first of two examples was
completed in March 1935, and one
subsequently reached a speed of
199.6km/h (124mph) on level track, a
performance which compares most
favourably with the Mallard's downhill
record of 202.9km/h (126mph).

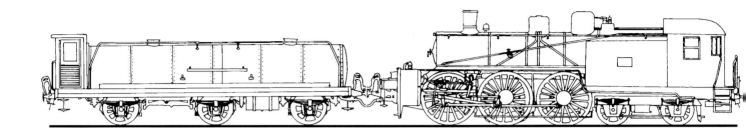

Italy was another European country where the original railways were built by the individual states, and where electrification began at an early stage. The unification of Italy was achieved only in 1870, and the old state systems continued to operate until after the First World War.

The frequently-quoted adage about the Italian railways that Mussolini made the trains run on time is as much a myth as might be expected. The credit actually belongs to Carlo Crova who, as the general manager of the new State system in the 1920s, was responsible for the old Adriatic, Mediterranean and Sicilian systems. Although he had succeeded in imposing order and punctuality on them, the Fascists happened to be handily placed at the time to take the credit.

Some unusual designs of locomotive have been operated on Italian railways. Among them was the Plancher type with the cab in front of the boiler, that was built in 1900 to make life easier for the crew in the narrow tunnels of

Above: *a Class 500 locomotive of the cab-in-front type, designed by Giuseppe Zara for the Adriatic System in 1900. This was a four-cylinder Plancher compound with two high-pressure cylinders (inside and out) on one side of the locomotive, and two low-pressure cylinders*

the Adriatic main line. Another cab-in-front design was produced in 1937 by Attilio Franco, whose concern was with improving boiler efficiency. Franco's ideas were developed by Piero Crosti into a distinctive type of boiler which carried the feed water tanks alongside the main boiler, and led the exhaust gases through these to the chimneys at the sides of the boiler.

Below: *one of the earliest compound locomotives to run in Spain was this superheated mixed-traffic 4–8–0. They started work on the Madríd, Zaragoza & Alicante (MZA) lines in 1914*

This boiler was used on a series of 83 modified locomotives of the 743 class among other Italian types, and was used on ten of the British Railways Class 9 standard type 2–10–0s. As with other innovations of this period, however, it appeared too late for a full evaluation of its worth. The extra complication of its construction and maintenance would probably have outweighed the savings of about 10% in fuel, except where coal was in short supply.

All the railway systems discussed so far have been of standard gauge at least on the main lines, but there are two areas of Europe where a different gauge was chosen. One of these is the Iberian peninsula, where the Spanish and Portuguese railways use a gauge of 1.676m (5ft 6in). The Spanish railways were initially built both by the various states and by private concerns, using imported locomotives. After the First World War, however, most Spanish locomotives were built on home territory, and in 1941 the railways were nationalised.

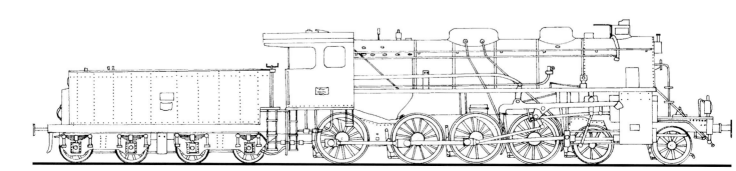

**RENFE 242F class No 2004 at
Burgos, May 1964**

Conditions on the Spanish railways can be compared with those in Austria. Long-distance routes involved many mountain sections, and the 4–8–0 configuration was adopted at an early stage. Subsequent designs typically have had eight coupled driving wheels, with two or four leading and trailing wheels. A distinctive example is the 242F class 4–8–4, a big and powerful type first built in 1955 and used to operate heavy passenger services.

The other European broad-gauge railway system is at the opposite end of the continent, where Finnish and Russian railways are built to the 1.524m (5ft) gauge. Finland had only about 4,830km (3,000 miles) of route and a correspondingly small number of locomotives, though steam locomotives continued in service there long after they had disappeared from other European lines. The two main classes developed were the Hr 1 Pacifics for passenger traffic, and the Tr 1 freight 2–8–2s.

Elsewhere in Scandinavia, the wide

availability of hydro-electric power led to electrification replacing steam, although at one time in Sweden numerous independent companies operated alongside the State system, and the variety of locomotive types was enormous.

India came to have one of the most varied railway systems in the world. Two standard gauge networks were built, termed broad and metre gauge respectively, and subsequently many narrower-gauge lines were added. Currently many millions of passengers a day are carried on Indian trains and the last steam locomotive was only taken out of service in 1997.

The Second World War saw the arrival in India of numbers of American locomotives supplied under Lend-Lease. The first examples of the new standard design of Pacifics, the Class WP, were ordered from Baldwin in the United States. Ultimately, a total of 755

WPs were built in a number of other countries as well as in India. The freight counterpart of the WP was the WG 2–8–2, and just as with the earlier classes there were metre-gauge YP and YG equivalents. Again, indigenous production was supplemented by large orders from other countries, and the total of WGs alone reached 2,450.

Shortly after Independence and Partition were achieved in 1947 and with them the separation of the railway system into Indian and Pakistani administrations, the introduction of new standard classes of locomotives began. The Pacific type had been selected by the Locomotive Standard Committee in the 1920s as permitting large fireboxes and grates suitable for quite low grades of coal, and light, intermediate and heavy designs of Classes XA, XB and XC were produced for working the broad-gauge lines. The corresponding YB Pacifics and ZB 2–6–2s were evolved for the metre and narrow-gauge lines, while for freight work XD and even bigger XE 2–8–2s

41

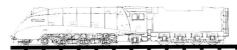

for the broad-gauge and smaller YD and ZE 2–8–2s for the other track gauges completed the range.

For all the achievements of the builders of the 64,000km (40,000-mile) Indian railway network, and of the administrators in running a transport system for so many people, the most famous of all India's railways is a little 0.61m (2ft) gauge line that twists its way from Siliguri up into the foothills of the Himalayas and the old hill station of Darjeeling.

Like Indian locomotives, Chinese engines display an attractive variety of ornamentation and decoration. One of the distinctive features of Chinese locomotives, inherited from Soviet designs, is the prominent casing on top of the boiler which encloses a steam pipe leading forward from the dome to a regulator box which is sited on the smokebox behind the chimney. This casing is also apparent on the JS (Liberation) 2–8–2 and RM (People) 4–6–2 classes.

In the South Pacific, steam railways in Australia and New Zealand are now in the hands of the many preservation

Left, above: *Class XD No 22486 at Basin Bridge in February 1981*

Left, below, *Classes WP No 7095 and WG 9649 left, photographed in 1986*

Above: *Chinese JS class No 5383 at Sanchazi in December 1989*

organisations, diesel and electric traction having taken over the main-line operations.

The Australian railways were slow to develop in the early stages. The sparse population concentrated in widely dispersed centres, and the separate colonial administrations in six different regions, resulted initially in the building of more or less local lines. More seriously, the early agreement on broad-gauge construction between Victoria, South Australia and New South Wales was broken when the latter changed to standard gauge. The other two states, having already ordered broad-gauge locomotives, went ahead with the agreed measure so that when the first railways opened in the 1850s there were two different gauges in use.

The situation became yet more complicated during the 1860s and 1870s, when the other states began building their first railways. Tasmania followed Victoria and South Australia in using the 1.6m (5ft 3in) gauge, but Queensland and Western Australia opted for economy of construction with yet a third gauge, this time of 1.067m (3ft 6in). Later on, this was also applied to the Tasmanian system and to some lines built in South Australia.

The consequence of all this variety in gauges was that Victoria and South Australia were the only two colonies with a common border and the same gauge of railway. Moreover, full advantage was taken of the narrow gauge's suitability for light track, relatively sharp grades and tight curves, so that subsequent development was restricted by the track within colonies as well as by gauge changes between them.

The immense variety of locomotives that appeared in Australia as imported models were supplemented by the various colonies' own production, is well represented by the numerous

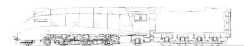

museums and preservation societies. The same is true of New Zealand, where argument over gauges hindered the early building of the railways.

The New Zealand rail authorities eventually standardised on a gauge of 1.067m (3ft 6in), and all lines were of this gauge by the end of the 1870s.

The locomotives of this period were predominantly tank types, but in 1874 the first J class Canterbury Goods 2–6–0 tender engines were built. A total of 32 of these were acquired, and the last was not withdrawn from service until 1955. The J class, like all locomotives used up to this period, were imported from England until the first indigenous types appeared.

In the early years of the twentieth century, typical products included the B, Ba and Bb 4–8–0 goods engines, of which a total of 50 were built. The majority were of the Bb type for passenger and mixed traffic as well as goods services.

In 1906 one of the most successful of all New Zealand steam locomotive designs appeared in the shape of the A class Pacific, a four-cylinder compound of the de Glehn type. A total of 57 were built, and after a long career on the express services, some were still at work on coal trains when steam was fully superseded by diesel power on the west-coast coal lines in 1969.

The Ab class was built in 1915 and used superheating to dispense with the ageing A class compound operation. It featured the novel Vanderbilt type of tender, which incorporated a large cylindrical water tank. A total of 141 were built, mostly in New Zealand, with further examples supplied by the North British Locomotive Company.

Later New Zealand types included the K class 4–8–4, designed to be the most powerful locomotive possible, given the rather restricted loading gauge on New Zealand lines. The original 30 Ks were supplemented by the improved Ka and Kb classes; the latter added a booster unit for use on the most heavily graded sections of the South Island.

For the lighter rails used on secondary lines, the J class 4–8–2s appeared in 1939. In their original form, the J class locomotives had an impressive style of

Above: *a New Zealand Railways Kc class 4–8–4 locomotive, which ran on the 1.07m (3ft 6in) gauge*

Below: *Rhodesian Railways 4–6–4+4–6–4 Garratt locomotive*

streamlined casing, though this was later removed and it was omitted entirely from the later Ja class. These were the last steam locomotives designed for New Zealand Railways, as the conversion to diesel operation began in 1948 with the first orders for diesel shunting engines, and the first main-line diesels followed two years later.

Early in the twentieth century, the Australian engineer Herbert Garratt had developed a new system of articulation. This involved mounting the water tank and fuel bunker on separate engine units fore and aft of the boiler, which

was carried between the two. As well as allowing the locomotive to pivot at two points, the Garratt system has a number of other advantages: a high adhesion weight is spread over a long wheelbase; a large diameter of boiler can be used; and the firebox grate can be deep and wide, since there are no wheels and axles underneath it to constrain its size. The Garratt system was developed by the British firm of Beyer, Peacock & Company Ltd, and the Beyer-Garratt locomotive proved ideal for African conditions as soon as it was introduced in South Africa shortly after the First World War.

Above: *the Little Nugget saloon car of the Union Pacific's* City of Los Angeles

Below: *New York Central's* Twentieth Century Limited *ran between New York and Chicago*

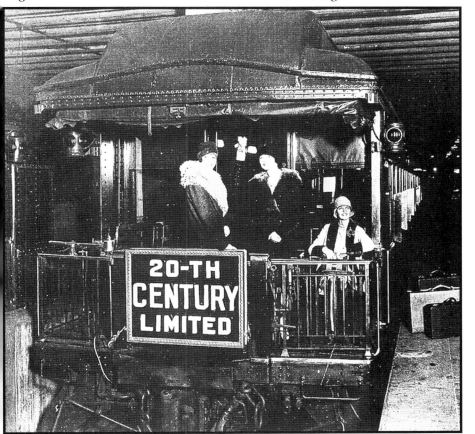

By the early part of the twentieth century, there were already a number of alternative routes across North America. James J. Hill, owner of the Northern Pacific and Great Northern lines, was able to complete the route from Chicago to Seattle and Portland by acquiring the Chicago, Burlington & Quincy Railroad and the most appropriately-named *Empire Builder* service was inaugurated in 1929.

During the 1930s many newly-named trains were introduced, in an effort to stem the loss of passengers resulting from the growing use of privately-owned motor cars and the economic depression that followed the stock market collapse of 1929. By that time the Chicago & Northwestern and the Union Pacific had eradicated the bottleneck at Omaha by co-operating to run the *City of San Francisco* and the *City of Los Angeles* services to California. The *City of Portland* and *City of Denver* served their respective cities, the latter connecting with the *California Zephyr* of the Denver & Rio Grande and Western Pacific railways.

None of these services did anything to eradicate the need for a change at Chicago, and during the 1930s the

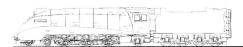

competition between the New York
Central and Pennsylvania railroads was
as fierce as ever. The respective prestige
services on the two lines at that time
were the *Twentieth Century Limited*
and the *Broadway Limited*. In 1910 the
Pennsylvania had opened its new
station in the centre of New York,
eliminating the need for passengers to
take a ferry from Manhattan Island to
Jersey City before beginning their rail
journeys, and by the 1930s both of the
railroads were running their fastest
trains to Chicago in 16 hours.

In the period between the two World
Wars, the North American passenger
train developed to its finest form. The
passenger cars were luxurious and the
services provided were lavish. The very
names of the trains were associated
with an aura of high romance and
adventure: *Empire Builder, Chief,
Daylight, Twentieth Century Limited*
and countless more became household
words.

The *Twentieth Century Limited*,
arguably the most famous of them all,
served the high-density 1,547km (961
miles) from New York to Chicago. It was
a joint venture, introduced in 1902 by
two railroads, the New York Central &
Hudson River Railroad and the Lake
Shore & Michigan Southern Railroad,
which later became amalgamated as
the New York Central system. The train
was first formed entirely of Pullman
cars, which could be converted to
sleepers at night.

The opening up of the western United
States by the transcontinental railroads
in the 1870s was mirrored in the
following decade by the building of the
Canadian Pacific. The construction of
a transcontinental railway in Canada

was a stipulation of the agreement by
which the formerly independent colony
of British Columbia became part of the
Canadian federation in 1871. The
original agreement was that the line
should be completed within ten years,
though it was another 15 years before
the first trains were running between
Montréal and the Pacific coast.

This was a formidable achievement,
however, in view of the succession of

mountain ranges in the west and the
combination of rock and swamp with

**Above: *the last spike is driven home
to complete the transcontinental
Canadian route, 7 November 1885***

**Below: *a Canadian National Railways
two-cylinder K-5 Hudson (4–6–4)
type, built by the Montréal
Locomotive Works from 1930***

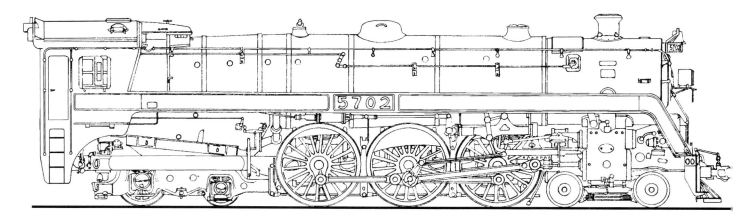

which the builders had to contend in their progress round the north of Lake Superior. The Canadian Pacific Railway grew to become one of the most successful rail operations in North America.

The other principal component of the Canadian railway system was Canadian National, which was formed after the First World War from a combination of government-owned lines and bankrupt private-enterprise systems. The competition between the two main systems helped to promote some excellent services on Canadian railways, and initiated some outstanding locomotive designs.

The early locomotives were generally of the American type 4–4–0, and for the services between Montréal and Ottawa Canadian Pacific produced an impressive design of the Atlantic type 4–4–2 in 1899. These were four-cylinder compound engines able to operate 77.3km/h (48mph) services, including intermediate stops, between the two cities.

The dominant problem in Canadian railway operations, however, has always been the western mountain ranges. To deal with the climb through the Kicking Horse Pass route, Canadian Pacific produced the first of its famous class of 2–10–4 Selkirks in 1929.

Contemporary with the Selkirks were the most famous of all Canadian locomotives, the Hudsons. These were 4–6–4 engines employed on passenger services and produced by the Montréal Locomotive Works, the same firm that built the Selkirks. They were at their most impressive on the Montréal to Ottawa services, where in the 1930s they worked some of the fastest schedules in the world.

BR class 9F No 92220 **Evening Star** *on the 15.40 train from Bournemouth to Bath near Wincanton, August 1962*

Evening Star

The British government nationalised the railway companies in 1948, naming the new amalgamated company as British Railways (BR). The last steam engine to have been built for BR was the appropriately named *Evening Star,* a versatile mixed- service locomotive capable of 144.9km/h (90mph).

Ten years after BR's announcement of its modernisation plan, the last regular steam-hauled passenger train left Paddington Station, London, on 11 November 1965. Three years later the last regular goods services to be operated by steam came to an end. The plan entitled *The Reshaping of British Railways* had been published already in 1962. As a consequence of this report BR's route mileage was reduced from over 27,370km (17,000 miles) in the year of publication to under 19,320km (12,000 miles) by 1970, while passenger stations were reduced from 743 to 299 over the same period.

GLOSSARY

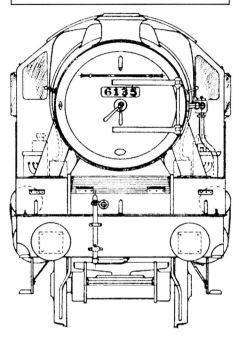

The Class 6F rebuilt Royal Scot

Adhesion: the frictional grip between locomotive wheel and rail.

Adhesive weight: the weight on the driving wheels of a locomotive; on its amount depends the frictional grip between wheels and rail.

Air brake: power braking system with compressed air as the operating medium.

Arch tubes: tubes connected to the water-space of the boiler provided in and across the firebox in order to increase high-temperature heating surface area. They also support the brick arch.

Articulated locomotive: a steam locomotive the driving wheels of which are in distinct sets, one or more of which are hinged or pivoted. Fairlie, Beyer-Garrett and Mallet are the major types.

Articulation: the sharing of one bogie by adjacent ends of two vehicles.

Ashpan: a feature of the locomotive which collects the ashes which fall through the bars of the grate.

Axlebox: the axle bearings of a locomotive are known as axleboxes. They are usually box-shaped to suit the guides and openings in the frames which should constrain movement in the horizontal plane

but allow freedom vertically.

Balancing: the reciprocation and revolving masses of any steam engine need balancing, if it is to work smoothly. Revolving masses can easily be balanced by counterweights, but the balancing of reciprocating parts is a matter of both compromise and judgment.

Banking: assisting the working of a train, usually when ascending a gradient, by attaching additional locomotives to the rear.

Bar frames: see *frames.*

Bearings: the bushing or metal block of anti-friction material which then transmits the load via an oil film to a journal.

Blast pipe: the exhaust pipes of a steam locomotive are arranged so that the steam emerges as a jet through a nozzle in the smokebox below the chimney. This creates a partial vacuum in the smokebox, which draws air through the boiler tubes and through the fire, thus enabling combustion to take place.

Blowdown valve: a way of releasing water, plus impurities contained therein, from the lowest water space of the boiler.

Blower: a steam jet in the smokebox or at the base of the chimney which can be used to draw up the fire when the locomotive is not being run under steam.

Bogie: (US *truck*) a pivoted truck, usually four wheeled, provided at the front or rear of a locomotive to give guidance and support. Most items of rolling stock are carried on bogies.

Boiler: steam-producing unit. The locomotive boiler consists essentially of a firebox surrounded by a water space in which the combustion of fuel takes place, and a barrel containing the flue tubes surrounded by water.

Boiler tubes: see *fire tubes.*

Bolster: transverse floating beam member of the bogie suspension system supporting the weight of the vehicle body.

Brakes: locomotives usually (but not always) have a hand brake and (also usually) some form of power brake. Power brakes can be actuated by compressed air, steam or vacuum. Air and vacuum brakes normally can be

applied throughout the train by using the controls on the locomotive.
Air brake: the commonest form of train brake, using compressed air as the medium of application.
Vacuum brake: the alternative to an air brake. For steam locomotives, the vacuum is much simpler than the air brake, mainly because a vacuum can be generated from any steam supply by a simple static ejector, whereas compressed air needs a relatively complex pump. The objection to the vacuum system is that the pressure available is limited to about three-quarters of the atmospheric pressure, thus providing only a limited brake force.

Brick arch: a brick or concrete baffle provided at the front of a locomotive firebox below the tubes, in order to extend the flame path. The early locomotives burnt coke; provision of a brick arch was necessary before it was possible to use coal without producing excessive smoke.

Cam: reciprocating, oscillating or rotating body which imparts motion to another body known as a follower, with which it is in contact.

Chimney: (US *smokestack*), the opening through which the exhaust steam and the gaseous products of combustion are dispersed into the atmosphere.

Clack valve or **check valve:** a non-return valve attached to the boiler at the points at which feed water is admitted.

Coal pusher: a steam-operated device in the tender, intended to push coal forward to a point where it can be shovelled directly into the fire.

Combustion chamber: a recessing of firebox tubeplate inside the boiler in order to increase the firebox volume at the expense of reducing the length of the tubes, so as to promote better combustion in long-barrelled boilers.

Compound: in a compound loco-motive, steam is made to work twice over, with consequent fuel savings. In the first high-pressure cylinder or cylinders, the steam is only partially expanded. This expansion is then completed and the residual energy extracted in a low-pressure cylinder or cylinders. The temperature gradient

within each cylinder is reduced considerably, and thus condensation losses are minimised. The high and low-pressure cylinders have to be arranged to do about the same quantity of work, and the low-pressure cylinders are normally of a greater diameter than the high-pressure cylinders, as the steam at low pressure occupies a greater volume.

Compressor: machine for raising the pressure of air above atmospheric; provides compressed air for operation of brakes, auxiliaries and so on.

Conjugated valve gear: more than two cylinders were often used in order to provide smoother running, and also where an adequate total cylinder volume could only be provided in this way. In order to reduce complication, the valves of all the cylinders could be arranged to be worked by conjugating levers from the valve gears of two of them.

Connecting rod: (US *main rod*) these connect the piston rods to the crank pins of the driving wheels or to the crankshaft.

Coupling rod: connects together the crank pins of the driving or coupled wheels on one side of a locomotive.

Counter-pressure brake: using the pumping action of the cylinders in order to brake the train. Great heat is generated and the cylinders are kept from overheating dangerously by the injection of water, which instantly flashes into steam, thereby absorbing the energy generated.

Crank: device for converting rotary to reciprocating motion or vice versa. It consists of an arm, one end of which is fixed to a shaft and the other free to rotate about the axis of the shaft.

Crank axles: the inside cylinders of locomotives drive onto axles with sections offset to form cranks.

Crank pins: locomotive wheels are driven by rods which transmit the driving force to the driving wheels through these large steel pins fixed in the wheels.

Crosshead: in conjunction with the guide-bars, the crosshead guides and constrains the piston rod to keep in line as it moves in and out of the cylinder.

Cut off: the point during the cylinder stroke at which steam is cut off by the valves. It is usually expressed as a percentage of that stroke.

Cylinders: in a steam locomotive the energy contained in steam is turned into mechanical force inside the cylinders. Each cylinder contains a piston and the pressure of the steam on this piston produces the force.

Dampers: the amount of heat that is produced by a fire is governed by the amount of air admitted to it. This can be adjusted by opening or closing damper doors in the locomotive's ashpan assembly. These are worked by levers situated in the locomotive cab.

Deflector dome: this is provided in or on the tender in connection with the water pick-up apparatus. Water first scooped from a set of troughs fitted between the rails is then fed skywards up a vertical pipe; the deflector dome at the top of this pipe then turns the flow downwards so that the tender is filled.

Down: usually the line of track which carries trains in a direction away from the town or city in which the railway company's headquarters are located; a train travelling in that direction.

Draincocks: when a locomotive is starting from cold, the first steam which enters the cylinders condenses to water. Draincocks are provided, worked from the cab, to allow this water to escape, otherwise the cylinder would be burst by the pressure of trapped water when the piston reached the end of its stroke.

Drawbar-horsepower/hour: a unit of work done by a locomotive when hauling a train. One of these units represents the exertion of a single horse-power at the locomotive drawbar for an hour.

Driving wheels: the driven wheels of a locomotive, sometimes referred to as coupled wheels.

The driving wheels and valve gear of SNCF Class 242.U1

Disc brake: braking mechanism utilising friction pads applied by calliper action to a disc secured to vehicle axle or wheel centre.

Dome: the steam is usually taken from the boiler at its highest point. Where height is available, a chamber known as the dome is provided above the top of the boiler barrel in order to collect the steam.

Double head: to attach a second locomotive to the front of a train.

Drop-grate or **dump-grate:** when disposing of a locomotive the fire residue was traditionally shovelled out through the fire-hole door, but an arrangement to allow the whole grate to be dropped or dumped was sometimes provided.

Eccentric: disc, keyed to a shaft or axle, the centre of which does not coincide with that of the axle. It rotates inside a ring, known as an eccentric strap, to which is attached

the eccentric rod, and imparts reciprocating motion to a link for operating the steam distribution valve to the cylinder.

Exhaust steam: emission of steam from the cylinder after completion of the working stroke.

Expansion of steam: increase in volume of steam in the cylinder after the supply has been cut off. An ability to take maximum advantage of the expansive qualities of steam results in economies in the consumption of fuel and water.

Feed-pump: a pump to feed water into the boiler; either driven from the motion or independently by steam from the boiler.

Firebox: the box in which the fire burns. It is made of steel or copper and fixed inside the boiler.

Fire door or **fire-hole door:** the entrance to the firebox, through which coal is shovelled, is closed off by a fire door.

Fire tubes: the hot gases from the fire pass through tubes in the boiler between the firebox and the smokebox, so heating the water with which they are surrounded.

Flange: projecting edge or rim on the periphery of a wheel or rail.

Flange lubricators: on sharp curves, wheel flanges bear heavily against the rails. In order to ease wear and reduce friction, devices to lubricate these flanges may be provided on the locomotive, but more usually they are attached to the rail.

Flues: large fire tubes, often referred to as superheater flues, which contain the superheater elements.

Footplate: the surface on which a locomotive crew stands. In fact it usually extends all round the engine, but the term is now taken to mean the floor of the driving cab.

Foundation ring: the rectangular fitting which connects the firebox to the boiler at the lowest point of both.

Frames or **mainframes:** the basic foundation on which the locomotive is constructed. In British practice, the frames are generally formed of plates; US practice originally favoured bars, but cast steel was used generally in later years.

Fusible plugs: a last-ditch defence

against the consequences of boiling the top of the firebox dry, consisting of screwed brass plugs each with a lead core. If there was no water present, the lead would melt and the leakage of steam would, to some extent, douse the fire.

Gauge: the distance between running edges or inner faces of the rails of railway track.

Grade or **gradient:** the slope of inclination to the horizontal of a railway; expressed in degrees from the horizontal, as a percentage, or unit rise or fall to the horizontal or slope length.

Grate: usually formed of cast-iron bars, on which the fire burns.

Gross weight: total weight of the train including payload.

Guide bars: see *crosshead*.

Handbrake: means of applying the brake blocks to the wheel treads without power assistance; usually in the form of a screwed shaft with a running nut, attached to the gearing.

Heating surface: areas of locomotive boiler exposed to heat on one side and available for water evaporation on the other.

Horns: these are guides, attached to the frames, in which the axleboxes can move vertically when running.

Horsepower: a unit of power; equal to 75kg metres per sec, 33,000ft per lb per min, or 746 watts.

Hot box: an overheated vehicle axlebox bearing resulting from the breakdown of the lubricating film between bearing and journal.

Indicated horsepower: the power developed inside the locomotive cylinders.

Injector: a static device for feeding water into the boiler by means of a series of cones. It is driven by a supply of live steam taken from the boiler or, in the case of an exhaust-steam injector, from the locomotive's exhaust when running.

Journal: area of a shaft or axle supported by a bearing.

Jumper blast-pipe: this device was sometimes attached to the blast-pipe in order to limit the draught when the engine was working hard.

Lead: the amount which a main steam port of a locomotive cylinder is open when the appropriate piston is at its limit of travel.

Life guard: provided in front of the leading wheels of a locomotive with the idea of throwing aside objects encountered on the rails; often also called a *guard iron*.

Light engine: locomotive running without a train.

Load factor: the ratio of actual train loading to maximum capacity.

Loading gauge: a railway's restrictive dimensions of height and width of rolling stock and loads carried to ensure adequate clearance with lineside structures.

Low-water alarm: an automatic device to warn the crew that boiler-water is getting dangerously low.

Main rod: see *connecting rod*.

Manganese steel liners: hardwearing lining surfaces used to minimise wear on the horns.

Motion: a generic term used to describe the moving parts, other than the wheels and axles, of the engine.

A Class 5700 pannier tank locomotive

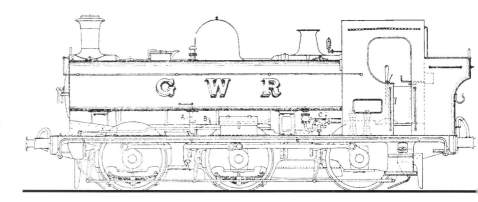

Motor bogie: bogie having driving wheels or motored axles.

Narrow gauge: railway track of less than the standard gauge.

Nosing: an oscillating movement of a locomotive about a vertical axis.

Packing: oil-absorbing material used to assist the lubrication of an axle bearing; also material placed in the gland to maintain a leak-free joint when subjected to pressure.

Pannier: a locomotive thjat has water tanks 'hung' on each side of the boiler.

Payload: that part of the total weight of the train which is revenue-earning, excluding the weight of empty vehicles and locomotive.

Piston: see *cylinders*.

Piston rod: the rod connecting the piston to the crosshead.

Piston valve: see *valves*.

Nominal rating: full load output of machine capable of being sustained for a continuous period of 12 hours without distress.

Poppet valve: see *valves*.

Port: see *valves*.

Priming: this occurs either when the water level in the boiler is too high or sometimes when impurities which cause foaming are present. It means that water is carried over down to the cylinders.

Push-pull: method of operating whereby the locomotive may be other than at the head of the train, although controlled from there.

Radial axles: provide the effect of a pony truck but without having a separate pivoted frame. The horns and axleboxes of a radial axle are made to allow sideways movement and are so constructed that such movement is sensibly radial about a vertical axis.

Regulator: (US *throttle*) serves the same purpose as the accelerator pedal on a car, though in the case of a locomotive it is a large and usually rather stiff steel handle.

Return crank: a revolving lever fixed on the end of a driving crank pin so that it provides the reciprocating motion, of correct magnitude and phase, to drive the valve gear.

Reversing lever: a lever used for the same purpose as the reversing wheel, but not often found on express passenger locomotives.

Reversing wheel or **reversing handle:** the wheel provided to alter the cut-off point of the valve gear and to move it between forward and reverse.

Rigid wheel base: horizontal distance between the centres of the first and last axles held rigidly in alignment with each other; the coupled wheels of a steam locomotive.

Rocking grate: an arrangement to enable the grate bars to be rocked or shaken, to encourage the residues of combustion to fall down into the ashpan.

Roller bearing: hardened steel cylinders located in a cage which revolve in contact with inner and outer races.

Round house: engine shed in which the locomotive stabling tracks radiate from a turntable.

Ruling gradient: limiting gradient, and therefore trainload, for traction and braking capacities.

Running gear: term generally applied to the wheels, axles, axleboxes, springs and frames of a railway vehicle.

Safety valves: allow steam to escape if pressure exceeds the safe limit.

Sanding gear: a device to put sand on the rails in order to improve wheel adhesion, particularly in damp conditions. It is worked from the cab, and the sand is either allowed to fall by gravity, or is sprayed into position with steam or compressed air.

Scavenge: to remove the waste products of combustion from an internal combustion engine cylinder by a regulated flow of air.

Shock absorber: telescopic hydraulic device, commonly used for damping spring suspensions.

Shoe brake: simple arrangement for applying a retarding or braking force to the periphery of rotating drum or wheel, by pressure of a block of wood, metal or friction material against it.

Sleeper: steel, wood or precast concrete beam for holding the rails to the correct gauge and distributing to the ballast the load imposed by passing trains.

Slide-bars: see *crosshead*.

Slide-valves: see *valves*.

Slip: loss of adhesion between driving wheel and rail, causing wheels to spin; also short curved connecting line joining lines which cross one another on the lever; also a driving member rotating at a higher speed than in a fluid coupling

Smokebox: a chamber at the front end of the boiler which serves to collect ashes drawn through the tubes. A partial vacuum formed in the smokebox by a jet of exhaust steam that emerges from the blast pipe provides a flow of air from and through the fire.

Snifting valves: these have the same function as normal bypass valves but function by admitting air to the steam circuit at an appropriate point when a vacuum is formed in them.

Spark arrester: a device in the smokebox or chimney to prevent sparks being thrown.

Splashers: provided to cover the portion of large driving wheels if they protrude through the footplate or running board.

Spring hangers: the tips of leaf springs on a steam locomotive are invariably connected to the frames by links known as spring hangers.

Standard gauge: 1,435mm (4ft 8.5in) in most of Europe and the major North American railways.

Stays: by its nature, the firebox of a locomotive cannot be circular like the front part of the boiler barrel. Its shape, therefore, needs retaining and this is done by a mass of rods known as stays, connecting the firebox to the boiler shell.

Stub axle: short, non-revolving axle which supports only one wheel.

Stuffing gland: where a moving piston rod emerges from a cylinder in which steam at high pressure is contained, a form of gland containing packing is needed to prevent leakage.

Superheating: the act of increasing the temperature and volume of steam after it leaves the boiler barrel by application of additional heat.

Suspension: the connecting system, including springs, between vehicle wheel and body, designed to give the best possible riding qualities by keeping unsprung weights to a minimum and reducing the shock

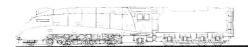

loadings on the track.

Swing-link: metal bar pivoted at each end; part of the suspension system of many bogies and trucks.

Tank locomotive: one which carries its fuel and water supplies on its own main frames.

Tender: a separate carriage for fuel and water, attached to a locomotive.

Tender locomotive: one which carries its fuel and/or water supplies in a separate semi-permanently coupled vehicle.

Thermal efficiency: the proportion of the heat value of the fuel consumed which appears as useful work.

Thermic syphon: vertical or near-vertical water ducts in the firebox provided with the idea of adding heating surface and improving circulation in the boiler.

Top feed: feed water is relatively cold and is best fed into the top of the boiler with clack or check valves fitted there, hence the term 'top feed'.

Tractive effort: this is a theoretical figure which indicates how hard a locomotive can pull when 85% (usually) of full-boiler pressure is applied to the pistons.

Train-pipe: continuous air to vacuum brake pipe, with flexible connections between vehicles, through which operation of the train brake can be controlled.

Traitement Intégral Armand (TIA): a form of water treatment, developed by Louis Armand of the French railways. It involved dosing the water in the tenders and regular tests of the acidity or alkalinity of the water in the boilers; it decimated boiler repair costs in France and elsewhere.

Trip: means of release by knocking aside a catch.

Tyre: (US *tire*) steel band forming the periphery of a wheel on which the flange and tread profile is formed.

Underframe: framework or structure which supports the body of a carriage or wagon.

Up line: line over which trains normally travel back towards the headquarters of the railway company concerned.

Up train: one which travels on or in the direction of the up line.

Vacuum: space from which air has been exhausted.

Valves: three types of valves were used on steam locomotives.
Slide valves were virtually universal during the first 75 years of steam construction. They consisted of a flat valve which slid on the flat port face in the steam chest. A recess in the valve face connected the exhaust port with one or other cylinder according to the position of the valve. Also, according to the position of the valve, one or other cylinder port was exposed by its edge as it moved in time with the movement of the piston; steam could then flow into the appropriate end of the cylinder.
Piston valves became virtually universal in the later years of steam. The steam chest was cylindrical; the boiler steam and exhaust steam were divided by two pistons which acted alternately to cover and uncover the cylindrical ports as the valves moved. The boiler steam could be admitted either in between or outside the pistons; these arrangements are known as *inside admission* or *outside admission* respectively, the former being the most usual one.
Poppet valves were used on a few steam locomotives, and were not dissimilar to those fitted to a car.

Valve gears: provided in order to move the valves of a locomotive to a precise timing in relation to the movement of pistons. It is necessary to cope with requirements for early and late cut off as well as forward and reverse working. Numerous linkages have been devised to do this. Walschaert's gear became almost universal in the later days of steam. Its working is as follows: a return crank is fixed to the main crank pin so that its little end revolves 90° out of phase with the main motion. By means of the eccentric rod, a curved slotted link is oscillated about a centre. A die-block which slides in this link is pivoted to the valve-rod. It can be lowered by the fore-and-aft movement of the eccentric rod, which is transmitted to the valve rod. If the lifting arm should be raised, the resultant movement of the valve rod is reversed. In this way, forward and

reverse timing of the valve is catered for. By a partial movement of the lifting arm, a reduced opening of the valve is provided. A combination lever serves to bias the opening of the valve towards the beginning of the stroke by, as it were, injecting a dose of the movement of the crosshead into the movement of the valve rod.
Baker's valve gear is derived from Walschaert's and replaces the curved slotted link with a series of plain links.
Stephenson's gear was used as universally as Walschaert's, which it preceded. Other gears such as Allan, 'gab' and Gooch were used in small numbers.

Variable gauge: vehicle or wheelset with facility for operating on more than one track gauge, achieved by sliding the wheel along the axle and locking it in the appropriate position to suit the required gauge.

Water gauge: a glass tube fixed to the boiler to allow the water level to be seen. This is the most important indication that there is on a steam locomotive and hence the gauge is usually duplicated.

Westinghouse brake: see *air brake*.

Yard: group of lines or sidings where auxiliary operations totrain working are undertaken.

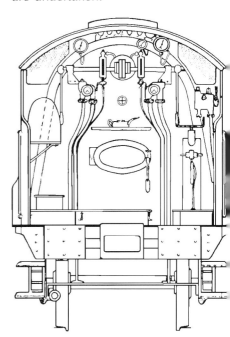

The cab of Class A3 Flying Scotsman

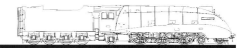

WHEEL NOTATION

Steam locomotives in Great Britain, the British Commonwealth and North America are described by a three-figure combination which refers to the number of wheels described in the sequence of the number of bogie, driving and trailing wheels. The first figure denotes the number of bogie wheels which are at the front of the locomotive.

In Europe the notation describes the number of wheels on one side of the locomotive only, and the driving wheels are represented by a letter, beginning with A for two driving wheels (one on each side), B for four (two on each side) and so on.

If a locomotive is a tank engine, a 'T' is appended to the third figure; if the locomotive is articulated, a fourth figure is included in the notation and the second and third figures refer to the driving wheels.

We have indicated the bogie wheels as solid black, the driving wheels as black open circles and the trailing wheels as a spoked circle in our illustrated examples.

UK/USA	Europe	Name
0–2–2	A1	
2–2–0	1A	Planet
2–2–2	1A1	Patentee
4–2–0	2A	Jervis
4–2–2	2A1	Bicycle
6–2–0	3A	Crampton
0–4–0	B	
0–4–2	B1	
2–4–0	1B	
2–4–2	1B1	Columbia
4–4–0	2B	American
4–4–2	2B1	Atlantic
4–4–4	2B2	Reading (Jubilee)
0–6–0	C	
0–6–2	C1	
0–6–4	C2	
2–6–0	1C	Mogul
2–6–2	1C1	Prairie
2–6–4	1C2	Adriatic
4–6–0	2C	Ten-wheeler
4–6–2	2C1	Pacific
4–6–4	2C2	Hudson (Baltic)
0–8–0	D	
0–8–2	D1	
2–8–0	1D	Consolidation
2–8–2	1D1	Mikado
2–8–4	1D2	Berkshire
4–8–0	2D	Mastodon
4–8–2	2D1	Mountain
4–8–4	2D2	Northern (Confederation)
6–8–6	3D3	Steam turbine
0–10–0	E	Decapod (UK)
0–10–2	E1	
2–10–0	1E	Decapod (USA)
2–10–2	1E1	Santa Fe
2–10–4	1E2	Texas
4–10–0	2E	Mastodon
4–10–2	2E1	Southern Pacific
4–12–2	2F1	Union Pacific
0–6–6–0	CC	Mallet articulated
2–4–4–2	1BB1	Mallet articulated
2–6–6–6	1CC3	Allegheny
2–8–8–4	1DD2	Yellowstone
4–6–6–4	2CC2	Challenger
4–8–8–4	2DD2	Big Boy
4–6–2 + 2–6–4	2C1+1C2	Garrett

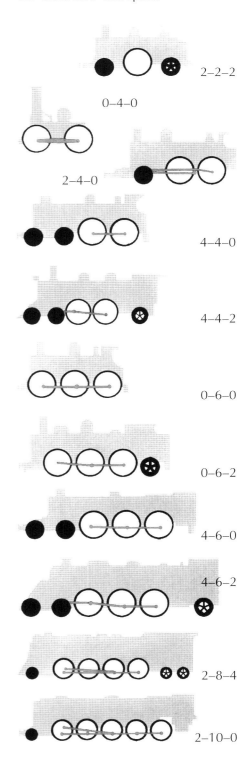

2–2–2

0–4–0

2–4–0

4–4–0

4–4–2

0–6–0

0–6–2

4–6–0

4–6–2

2–8–4

2–10–0

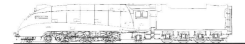

A CENTURY OF LOCOMOTIVES

AMERICAN TYPE 4–4–0

Country of origin: USA
Railway: Western & Atlantic Railroad (W&ARR)
Date: 1855
Length overall: 15.926m (52ft 3in)
Total weight: 40,909kg (90,000lb)
Cylinders: two 381 x 610mm (15 x 24in)
Driving wheels: 1.524m (5ft)
Axle load: 9,525kg (21,000lb)
Fuel: 7.25m³ (256cu ft) wood
Grate area: 1.35m² (14.5sq ft)
Water: 5,262 litres (1,250 Imp gal/ 2,000 US gal)
Heating surface: 91m² (980sq ft)
Steam pressure: 6.35kg/cm² (90psi)
Adhesive weight: 19,545kg (43,000lb)
Tractive force: 3,123kg (6,885lb)

This Currier & Ives print shows two American t ype 4–4–0 locomotives, of which some 25,000 were built

The image of a 4–4–0 locomotive crossing the boundless prairie at the head of a mixed train became a symbol of America's expansion westwards, from the mid-1800s. It was used by all of the railroads for more than 30 years, hauling every sort of train, and among its evident qualities were versatility and adaptability to heavy loads on all routes, simple construction and ready maintenance. The story of the Type in all its fascinating technical, social and military aspects was crucial to the conquest of the West, as railroads expanded rapidly in the 1850s.

The *General* was built by Thomas Rogers of Paterson, New Jersey, in 1855.

It has a long wheelbase for the bogies, which permitted the cylinders to be both horizontal and clear of the wheels. This also allowed direct attachment to the bar frames. Its average speeds were not high, at about 40km/h (25mph).

At Big Shanty, about 48km (30 miles) north of Atlanta, the fabled *General* was hijacked by a group of Union soldiers who had infiltrated into Confederate territory during the American Civil War. They were chased for eight hours by two other American Type 4–4–0s, *Yonah* and *Texas*, at speeds of up to 100km/h (60mph), on a single track, before the *General* ran out of fuel.

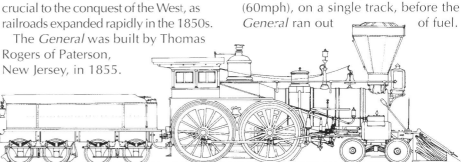

MÉDOC CLASS 2–4–0

Country of origin: Switzerland
Railway: Swiss Western railway
Date: 1857
Length overall: not known
Total weight: 40,000kg (88,400lb)
Cylinders: two 408 x 612mm (16 x 24in)
Driving wheels: 1.69m (5ft 6.25in)
Axle load: 9,200kg (20,150lb)
Fuel: 2,400kg (5,280lb)
Grate area: 1m² (10.75sq ft)
Water: 4,000 litres (880 Imp gal/ 1,050 US gal)
Heating surface: 95m² (1,023sq ft)
Superheater: none
Steam pressure: 8kg/cm² (114psi)
Adhesive weight: 18,100kg (40,000lb)
Tractive force: 4,077kg (8,986lb)

Right: a German-built Swiss Western railway long-boiler type, Médoc class 2–4–0

Although the Stephensons had established the rudiments of the steam locomotive it was to be others such as Forrester, Norris, Crampton, Borsig and others who were quicker to experiment and fine-tune what had become the final arrangement of the cylinders.

As a result, the haycock firebox had replaced the dome in the long boiler engines.

Following an accident in Germany in 1853, the 2–2–2 type locomotive was banned, and replaced by the 2–4–0. In France, however, the 2–4–0 had been introduced at once. Their principal user was the *Chemins de Fer de l'Ouest* (Ouest) which called

these long boiler engines the Médoc class, and this was almost a standard type of the period in France.

Those for the Swiss Western Railway, later known as the Jura-Simplon Railway, were built between 1856 and 1858 at Karlsruhe while Ernest-Alexandre Gouin was a major supplier to the French railways. The Ouest was equipped by Gouin with 122 locomotives of the 2–4–0 type between 1857 and 1880, and a further 327 similar locomotives between 1900 and 1901.

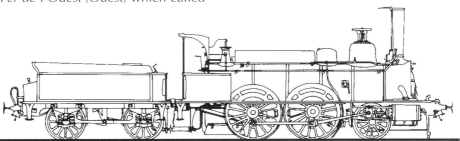

PROBLEM CLASS 2–2–2

Country of origin: UK
Railway: London & North Western Railway (LNWR)
Date: 1862
Length overall: 13.31m (43ft 8in)
Total weight: 60,500kg (133,000lb)
Cylinders: two 406 x 610mm (16 x 24in)
Driving wheels: 2.32m (7ft 9in)
Axle load: 15,000kg (33,000lb)
Fuel: 5,000kg (11,000lb)
Grate area: 1.39m² (15sq ft)
Water: 8,280 litres (1,800 Imp gal/ 2,160 US gal)
Heating surface: 102m² (1,097sq ft)
Superheater: none
Steam pressure: 8.54kg/cm² (150psi)
Adhesive weight: 12,000kg (26,500lb)
Tractive force: 4,458kg (9,827lb)

Above right: the LNWR Problem class Lady of the Lake was originally built in 1862, and is shown here with a rebuilt cab. There were 60 in the class which were contemporaries of Ramsbottom's Caledonian engines, the final example being built in 1865

Also known as the Lady of the Lake class, these locomotives were built by John Ramsbottom at Crewe to the instructions of the directors of the London & North-Western Railway (LNWR). They wanted a locomotive that was cheap both to build and to operate.

For this reason, the Problem class relied upon simplicity. They had no outside frame and no bogies, the leading axle being carried in the frame like the others.

The outside-cylinder, inside-valve arrangement was extremely basic and after the tenth to be built, the Gifford injector replaced pumps for feeding the boiler.

The Problems were used for

hauling the Irish Mail trains from Euston to Holyhead, changing engines at Stafford. A Problem ran from Holyhead to Stafford, a distance of 210km (130 miles), at an average speed of about 87km/h (54mph). This non-stop run was made possible only by Ramsbottom's invention of the water trough, which allowed water to be picked up while the locomotive was running at speed.

All of the class were rebuilt to the specification that appears here between 1895 and 1899, to incorporate new boilers and larger fireboxes. This resulted in an increase in weight of about 25%. All examples of the class were broken up about ten years later.

STIRLING 8ft SINGLE CLASS 4–2–2

Country of origin: UK
Railway: Great Northern Railway (GNR)
Date: 1870
Length overall: 15.24m (50ft 2in)
Total weight: 66,136kg (145,500lb)
Cylinders: two 457 x 711mm (18 x 28in)
Driving wheels: 2.463m (8ft 1in)
Axle load: 15,454kg (34,000lb)
Fuel: 3,409kg (7,500lb)
Grate area: 1.64m² (17.65sq ft)
Water: 13,369 litres (2,900 Imp gal/ 3,480 US gal)
Heating surface: 108m² (1,165sq ft)
Superheater: none
Steam pressure: 9.8kg/cm² (140psi)
Adhesive weight: 15,727kg (34,600lb)
Tractive force: 5,101kg (11,245lb)

GNR No 1 was a Stirling 4–2–2 and is shown here with its train of teak four-wheelers at Peterborough station in September 1938

Patrick Stirling was the locomotive superintendent of the Great Northern Railway (GNR), and ordered the first of these 2.438m (8ft) singles to be built in the line's own Doncaster works. A total of 47 examples of the class were built during a period of 23 years. They were locomotives of beautiful lines, which were emphasised by their paint and brass work.

The domeless boiler was unusual for the time, and it was to become a Stirling trademark. The engines were otherwise simple, with outside cylinders and inside valve chests with the slide valves being driven by sets of Stephenson's link motion.

These locomotives took the Edinburgh express from the King's Cross terminal in London with considerable loads, which they hauled at speeds of up to 120km/h (75mph). The class disappeared following the introduction of eight and twelve-wheeled bogie stock, corridor cars and dining cars. Thus the 8ft Singles were demoted to lesser tasks, and all had been withdrawn by 1916; however, the locomotive No 1 is still preserved at the National Railway Museum in York.

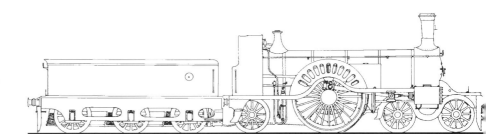

PRECEDENT CLASS 2–4–0

Country of origin: UK
Railway: London & North Western Railway (LNWR)
Date: 1874
Length overall: not known
Total weight: 32,900kg (72,500lb)
Cylinders: two 431 x 609mm (17 x 24in)
Driving wheels: 2.03m (6ft 8in)
Axle load: not known
Fuel: not known
Grate area: 1.6m² (17.1sq ft)
Water: not known
Heating surface: 100m² (1,083sq ft)
Superheater: none
Steam pressure: 9.8kg/cm² (140psi)
Adhesive weight: not known
Tractive force: 4,720kg (10,400lb)

Right: Webb's Precursor class, also of LNER, and far right, his Precedent class locomotive; both were built in 1874

Francis Webb took over from John Ramsbottom at the London & North Western Railway (LNWR) in 1871, and he ordered further locomotives of the same type as the *Samson* and *Newton* classes to be built. They were all painted black with polished brass nameplates, as was customary on that line, and were lined out in red and white.

First there were 70 *Precedent* type, with cylinders of 431 x 609mm (17 x 24in), driving 2.03m (6ft 8in) wheels. In order to supplement the class for duty on the heavily-graded lines between Crewe and Carlisle, there were also 40 engines of the *Precursor* class, similar to the Precedent class but

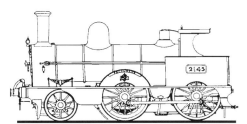

with driving wheels of 1.68m (5ft 6in).

Finally, there were the 96 engines of the Improved Precedent class, of which the last was built in 1894. It was one of these, No 790 *Hardwicke*, which took part in the final night of the race to Aberdeen on 21 August 1895, when it ran the 227km (141 miles) from Crewe to Carlisle in two hours and six minutes, at an average speed of 108km/h (67mph).

Hardwicke has been restored at the Steamtown Museum and is now on exhibition at the National Railway Museum, York.

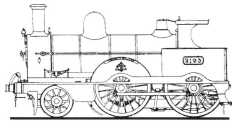

Below: *Precedent class No. 790 Hardwicke, as preserved at York*

DUKE CLASS 4–4–0

Country of origin: UK
Railway: Highland Railway (HR)
Date: 1874
Length overall: 15.61m (51ft 3in)
Total weight: 73,500kg (161,500lb)
Cylinders: two 457 x 610mm (18 x 24in)
Driving wheels: 1.92m (6ft 3.5in)
Axle load: 14,250kg (31,500lb)
Fuel: 4,000kg (8,800lb)
Grate area: 1.51m² (16.25sq ft)
Water: 8,280 litres (1,800 Imp gal/2,160 US gal)
Heating surface: 114m² (1,228sq ft)
Superheater: none
Steam pressure: 9.84kg/cm² (140psi)
Adhesive weight: 27,000kg (59,500lb)
Tractive force: 5,597kg (12,338lb)

Below: Duke class No 3256 Guinevere at Newbury with the stopping train to Southampton in April 1939

At the time of their introduction in 1874, the Duke class locomotives were the most powerful in Britain, designed to climb without fuss across their mountainous routes around Scotland.

Built by Dübbs to a design of Highland Railway's (HR) locomotive superintendent, David Jones, they were the first in a series of similar class locomotives which included the Clyde Bogie and the Strath classes, and totalled a fleet of 30.

Hard-working and proficient, the Dukes cut journey times and d d so with heavier loads. One example of this is the route from Perth to Inverness, a distance of 230km (143 miles), which in pre-Duke days took

five and a quarter hours. This was reduced to just four hours by the Dukes.

The class was the first to exhibit the HR hallmark of a louvred chimney, which drew the steam exhaust up clear of the cab and also yielded more efficient draughting.

Alexander Allen's straight link valve gear was incorporated in the design, as were a double frame arrangement and La Châtelier's counter-pressure brake. The latter enabled the cylinders also to be employed to provide brake pressure.

The last Duke to survive had been also the first of the class, and it was withdrawn in 1923.

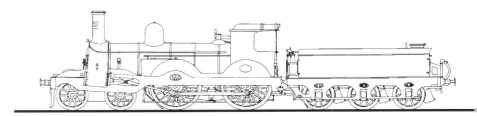

GLADSTONE CLASS 0–4–2

Country of origin: UK
Railway: London, Brighton &
Coast Railway (LBSCR)
Date: 1882
Length overall: 15.8m (51ft 10in)
Total weight: 69,500kg (153,000lb)
Cylinders: two 464 x 660mm (18.25
x 26in)
Driving wheels: 1.98m (6ft 6in)
Axle load: 14,750kg (32,500lb)
Fuel: 4,000kg (8,800lb)
Grate area: 1.88m² (20.3sq ft)
Water: 10,200 litres (2,240 Imp gal/
2,700 US gal)
Heating surface: 139m² (1,492sq ft)
Superheater: none
Steam pressure: 9.8kg/cm² (140psi)
Adhesive weight: 29,000kg
63,500lb)
Tractive force: 5,993kg (13,211lb)

Above right: No 199 Samuel Laing

*Below: No 216 Gladstone at the
NRM, York*

This was a class of express passenger locomotives, the culmination of a series of engines designed by William Stroudley as part of his reorganisation of the London, Brighton and South Coast Railway (LBSCR). At the time of his appointment, the railway had been running a hotchpotch of dissimilar and individual stock.

The Gladstone class locomotives were built at the LBSCR's Brighton

works over a period of eight years, with the class running to 36 examples.

The class had side valves placed under the cylinders with their port faces inclined, to enable the Stephenson's valve gear to work them directly without the intervention of rocking levers. Leaf springs were used on the leading axles, with coil springs on the centre axle.

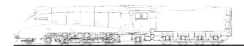

MIDLAND JOHNSON SINGLE 4–2–2

Country of origin: UK
Railway: Midland Railway (MR)
Date: 1887
Length overall: 16.038m (52ft 7.5in)
Total weight: 82,500kg (181,500lb)
Cylinders: two 483 x 660mm (19 x 26in)
Driving wheels: 2.375m (7ft 9.5in)
Axle load: 17,954kg (39,500lb)
Fuel: 4,000kg (8,800lb)
Grate area: 1.82m² (19.6sq ft)
Water: 15,902 litres (3,500 Imp gal/ 4,200 US gal)
Heating surface: 115m² (1,237sq ft)
Superheater: none
Steam pressure: 12kg/cm² (170psi)
Adhesive weight: 17,950kg (39,500lb)
Tractive force: 6,582kg (14,506lb)

The restored Midland Railway Johnson Single No 673 at Butterley, July 1977

The Midland Railway specialised in fast, light locomotives, and introduced the first of its Johnson-designed single-wheelers in 1887. The fleet had grown to 95 by the end of the century. The original driving wheels measured 2.23m (7ft 4in) across, but by the time the last examples were built in 1900 this had increased to 2.37m (7ft 9.5in). The class was built in several batches, with minor modifications having been incorporated along the way. The Midland Railway had appointed Samuel Waite Johnson as its locomotive superintendent in 1873.

The application of steam sanding gear in 1885 caused the side rods of some of the Midland 2–4–0 engines to be removed, and they then worked satisfactorily with only one driving axle. This heralded the return of the single-wheelers, or 'Spinners' as they had become known.

The Midland Johnson Singles operated fairly successfully, regularly hauling express trains of between 203.2 and 254 tonnes (200 and 250 tons), or more in good weather and recording speeds of up to 144km/h (90mph). Today, the one which is still preserved is on exhibition at Derby. It was built in 1897, and No 118 remained in service until 1928.

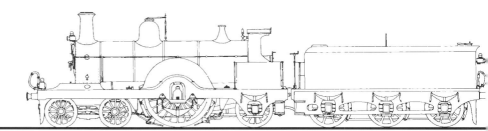

TEUTONIC CLASS 2–2–2–0

Country of origin: UK
Railway: London & North Western Railway (LNWR)
Date: 1889
Length overall: 15.55m (51ft 0.25in)
Total weight: 72,000kg (158,000lb)
Cylinders: two 356 x 610mm (14 x 24in) high pressure; one 762 x 610mm (30 x 24in) low pressure
Driving wheels: 2.16m (7ft 1in)
Axle load: 16,000kg (35,000lb)
Fuel: 5,000kg (11,000lb)
Grate area: 1.9m² (20.5sq ft)
Water: 8,179 litres (1,800 Imp gal/2,160 US gal)
Heating surface: 130m² (1,402sq ft)
Steam pressure: 12.3kg/cm² (175psi)
Adhesive weight: 31,500kg (69,500lb)

At one time, the London & North Western Railway was the largest joint-stock corporation in the world, and the works at Crewe unbelievably self-sufficient, capable of building the fleetest of locomotives.

Francis Webb was the man responsible for the locomotive works, who had built his reputation with a series of 2–4–0 non-compound engines which included *Hardwicke*.

Webb experimented with compounding, and adopted a system of two outside high-pressure cylinders which drove the rear driving wheels, and a single exceptionally large low-pressure cylinder to drive the front driving axle. There was an absence of coupling gear, but there were three sets of Joy's valve gear. The prototype was No 66 *Experiment*, which was built in 1882, and this was followed by a batch of 29 examples built between 1883 and 1884. A second batch of 40, which were known as

the Dreadnought class, were built between 1884 and 1888. Both classes were undistinguished, difficult to start though they ran economically.

The best of the Webb compounds arrived in 1889, in the form of the Teutonic class locomotives. On these, the Joy's valve gear was replaced by a slip-eccentric, but the locomotives still experienced trouble in starting. The ten Teutonic class engines were very good once they did get going, however, creating a reputation for themselves by hauling the Scottish expresses from Euston as far as Crewe during the 1890s.

Below: *Webb's LNWR 2–2–2–0 experimental compound locomotive No 519* Shooting Star, *in 1901*

No 999 4-4-0

Country of origin: USA
Railway: New York Central & Hudson River Railroad (NYC&HRRR)
Date: 1893
Length overall: 17.63m (57ft 10in)
Total weight: 38,181kg (84,200lb)
Cylinders: two 483 x 610mm (19 x 24in)
Driving wheels: 2.184m (7ft 2in)
Axle load: 19,091kg (42,000lb)
Fuel: 7,000kg (15,400lb)
Grate area: 2.85m² (30.7sq ft)
Water: 13,393 litres (2,950 Imp gal/ 3,500 US gal)
Heating surface: 179m² (1,927sq ft)
Steam pressure: 12.6kg/cm² (190psi)
Adhesive weight: 38,181kg (84,000lb)
Tractive force: 7,382kg (16,270lb)

The record-breaking achievements of No 999 when hauling the Empire State Express have always been regarded as dubious. A conductor claimed that he timed a speed of 180km/h (112.5mph) down a 0.29% (one in 350) grade near Batavia, New York State, while the locomotive hauled four wagons each of between 50.8 and 55.9 tonnes (50 and 55 tons), on 10 May 1893. Another claim was made for a speed of 166km/h (102.8mph) timed over a posted 8km (five miles) of track during the previous night. Neither of these have been verified.

William Buchanan was the designer of No 999, and on its tender it carried the name of the train it

The preserved No 999 at the Chicago Museum of Science and Industry. Although painted in the same style as when it was built, the original 2.184m (7ft 2in) wheels have been replaced by these of 2.006m (6ft 7in)

hauled, the Empire State Express. Large driving wheels were a conspicuous feature of the locomotive, although when it was rebuilt, smaller wheels were substituted. The locomotive is now on display at the Chicago Museum of Science and Industry.

The Empire State Express ran between New York and Chicago during the time of the Colombian Exposition, completing the 1,536km (960-mile) journey in 20 hours. It introduced an unprecedented combination of speed and comfort for any comparable journey, and was the forerunner of the famous train, the Twentieth Century Limited, which later ran daily between the two cities

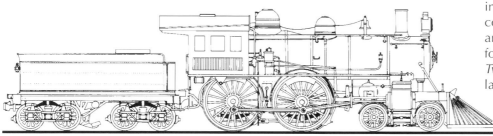

CLAUD HAMILTON CLASS 4–4–0

Country of origin: UK
Railway: Great Eastern Railway (GER)
Date: 1900
Length overall: 16.28m (53ft 4.75in)
Total weight: 97,000kg (213,000lb)
Cylinders: two 483 x 660mm (19 x 26in)
Driving wheels: 2.13m (7ft)
Axle load: 18,500kg (41,000lb)
Fuel: 3.25m³ (715 Imp gal/860 US gal) oil
Grate area: 2m² (21.3sq ft)
Water: 16,000 litres (3,450 Imp gal/4,150 US gal)
Heating surface: 151m² (1,631sq ft)
Steam pressure: 12.7kg/cm² (180psi)
Adhesive weight: 37,500kg (82,000lb)
Tractive force: 7,757kg (17,100lb)

Claud Hamilton at Yarmouth South Town shed, May 1956. The original batch of 41 locomotives remained in service until 1931. After rebuilding the class was not finally withdrawn until 1958

The first new engine of the twentieth century from the Great Eastern Railway's Stratford works was the superb 4–4–0 locomotive No 1900, *Claud Hamilton.* It featured an inside-cylinder layout, power-operated reversing gear, a water scoop, a blast-pipe with a variable opening and a very large cab with four windows.

Initially it was built to burn waste oil residues from the company's oil-gas plant. The class was built between 1900 and 1923, and there were 121 locomotives in the class.

The first batch had two sets of Stephenson's valve gear, which filled the remaining space left after two sets of main motion had been placed between the frames. Later batches had enlarged boilers,

superheaters and piston valves which replaced the earlier slide valves.

As improvements were made over the years, earlier batches were updated to conform with the final batch of 10 locomotives, built in 1923 and known as Super Clauds.

They were used as prime express locomotives to haul the 14-car *Norfolk Coast Express* of over 406.4 tonnes (400 tons) from London's Liverpool Street terminus to North Walsham. The schedule was two hours 39 minutes, for the non-stop journey of 208km (130 miles). They also hauled the Royal Trains to Sandringham, long after having been withdrawn from their *Norfolk Coast Express* duty.

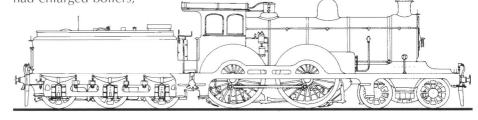

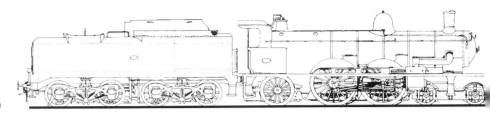

DE GLEHN ATLANTIC 4–4–2

Country of origin: France
Railway: Nord (Northern) railway
Date: 1901
Length overall: 18.25m (59ft 10.5in)
Total weight: 120,000kg (264,500lb)
Cylinders: two 340 x 640m (13.5 x 25.5in) high pressure; two 560 x 640m (22 x 25.5in) low pressure
Driving wheels: 2.04m (6ft 8.25in)
Axle load: 17,800kg (39,231lb)
Fuel: 7,000kg (15,000lb)
Grate area: 2.75m² (33.4sq ft)
Water: 23,000 litres (5,070 Imp gal/6,080 US gal)
Heating surface: 138m² (1,485sq ft)
Superheater: 39m² (420sq ft)
Steam pressure: 16kg/cm² (228psi)
Adhesive weight: 35,600kg (78,500lb)
Tractive force: 120,000kg (264,500lb)

A de Glehn four-cylinder compound 4–4–2 No 2.670 as restored and exhibited at the Musée Français du Chemin de Fer *(French National Railway Museum), Mulhouse*

Alfred de Glehn, an Englishman, was appointed director of engineering at the *Société Alsacienne de Constructions Méchaniques* at Mulhouse. In conjunction with Gaston du Bousquet of the Nord (Northern) railway, he developed a system of compounding for steam locomotives. Their four-cylinder type was to stand the test of time, and provided the basis for the majority of French express locomotives for the remaining days of steam.

However, the de Glehn system was extremely complicated, with two sets of reversing gear and two throttles, in addition to intercepting valves to control the working.

The first example of the class was No 2.641, exhibited at the Paris Exhibition of 1900. It was to be the first of a batch of 32, built for the Nord, which were employed on the arduous boat train route between Paris and Calais. They showed a remarkable economy of coal consumption, and also were able to haul these trains of some 274 tonnes (270 tons) at speeds of 100km/h (60mph), up the 21km (13 miles) of 0.5% (one in 200) gradient between St Denis and Sarvilliers.

So impressive were the feats of these Atlantics that orders were received not only from the French railways for 59 units, but for a further 93 units from elsewhere around the world, from Egypt to North America.

LARGE ATLANTIC CLASS 4–4–2

Country of origin: UK
Railway: Great Northern Railway (GNR)
Date: 1902
Length overall: 17.634m (57ft 10.25in)
Total weight: 114,772kg (252,500lb)
Cylinders: two 508 x 610mm (20 x 24in)
Driving wheels: 2.032m (6ft 8in)
Axle load: 20,454kg (45,000lb)
Fuel: 6,560kg (14,500lb)
Grate area: 2.88m² (31sq ft)
Water: 15,890 litres (3,500 Imp gal/ 4,200 US gal)
Heating surface: 182.5m² (1,965sq ft)
Superheater: 52.8m² (568sq ft)

Steam pressure: 12kg/cm² (170psi)
Adhesive weight: 40,909kg (90,000lb)
Tractive force: 7,865kg (17,340lb)

Although modern in their design characteristics, the large Atlantics were nevertheless simple, with outside cylinders and Stephenson's valves and valve gear inside.

The first batch of 81 units to be built were unsuperheated and featured balanced slide valves, but

Below: *a 1908-built GNR Atlantic, and* **bottom,** *No 4451 on a down at Brookmans Park in 1937*

the final 10 units, which were built in 1910, had piston valves and superheaters. The earlier units were then upgraded.

The locomotives had been designed by Henry Ivatt and, with the exception of a single unit, all were built at the Great Northern Railway's (GNR) own Doncaster plant. It was these engines that introduced to Britain the big boiler with a wide firebox.

They were used to work the GNR section, as far north as York, of the east coast main line from London to Scotland. However, they were eventually stood down, the first ceasing to be worked in 1943 and the last surviving until November 1950.

MIDLAND COMPOUND 4–4–0

Country of origin: UK
Railway: Midland Railway (MR)
Date: 1902
Length overall: 17.26m (58ft 7.5in)
Total weight: 106,000kg (234,000lb)
Cylinders: one 483 x 660mm (19 x 26in) high pressure; two 533 x 660mm (21 x 26in) low pressure
Driving wheels: 2.13m (7ft)
Axle load: 20,500kg (44,500lb)
Fuel: 5,750kg (12,500lb)
Grate area: 2.63m² (28.4sq ft)
Water: 15,890 litres (3,500 Imp gal/ 4,200 US gal)
Heating surface: 122.5m² (1,317sq ft)
Superheater: 25.3m² (272sq ft)
Steam pressure: 14.1kg/cm² (200psi)
Adhesive weight: 40,500kg (89,000lb)

Above right: *one of the first group of 30, which were numbered 1000 to 1029*

Below: *preserved No 1000 at Rugby Central with the* **East Midlander,** *September 1960*

William Worsdell's No 1619, a London & North-Eastern F class, was rebuilt to the design of W.M. Smith in 1898. The rebuilt locomotive was a three-cylinder machine, having one high-pressure and two low-pressure cylinders. This design was taken up by Samuel Johnson of the Midland Railway, who produced five of these Midland Compounds. They were developed by his successor, Richard Deeley, and later substantially rebuilt by Henry Fowler; they were the only truly successfully compounded British locomotives.

When the Midland Railway amalgamated with others to form the London, Midland and Scottish (LMS) in 1923, it was this class of compound locomotive that was selected to be the basis of the standard express locomotive. In consequence, a total of 240 engines were built. Most of them survived for long enough to become British Railways (BR) locomotives, when they were renumbered from 40900 to 41199.

The majority had been built at Midland's Derby works; they were finally withdrawn from service in 196?

SAINT CLASS 4–6–0

Country of origin: UK
Railway: Great Western Railway (GWR)
Date: 1902
Length overall: 19.209m (63ft 0.25in)
Total weight: 114,090kg (251,000lb)
Cylinders: two 470 x 762mm (18.5 x 30in)
Driving wheels: 2.045m (6ft 8.5in)
Axle load: 18,863kg (41,500lb)
Fuel: 6,136kg (13,500lb)
Grate area: 2.52m² (27.1sq ft)
Water: 15,890 litres (3,500 Imp gal/ 4,200 US gal)
Heating surface: 171m² (1,841sq ft)
Superheater: 24.4m² (263sq ft)
Steam pressure: 15.8kg/cm² (225psi)
Adhesive weight: 56,818kg (125,000lb)
Tractive force: 11,066kg 24,395lb)

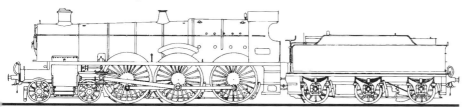

The broad gauge was abandoned by the Great Western Railway (GWR) in 1892, and the company's first 4–6–0 was produced at its Swindon works three years later. Before the century was out, George Jackson Churchward replaced William Dean as its chief locomotive engineer. Swindon then produced a big outside-cylinder 4–6–0, No 100, in 1902 and this followed the layout of the American ten-wheeler type of the Pennsylvania Railroad.

Both the cylinders and the valve chests were not only mounted outside the frames but were in the most accessible possible position. Inside the frames, the Stephenson's valve gear drove the inside-admission valves via transverse shafts and pendulum cranks. This was the basic arrangement that Churchward went on to use on some 2,000 locomotives.

Before the first named Saint locomotive appeared in 1907, 32 of the class had already been built following the second prototype of 1903. The first production batch of 19 examples had appeared in 1905, of which some ran for a time as 4–4–2s and were named after characters in Sir Walter Scott's Waverley novels. The next batch to produced in 1906 were named after ladies, and included *Lady Superior*, the first British locomotive to have a modern superheater. The next batch of 20 genuine Saint locomotives followed in 1907, and the first to be named was No 2911 *Saint Agatha*. These in turn were followed by 25 Courts, which were all superheated.

Red-backed plates showing on No 2934 Butleigh Court, ex-works at Swindon in June 1950

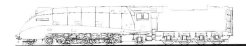

CITY CLASS 4–4–0

Country of origin: UK
Railway: Great Western Railway (GWR)
Date: 1903
Length overall: 17.126m (56ft 2.25in)
Total weight: 94,091kg (207,000lb)
Cylinders: two 457 x 660mm (18 x 26in)
Driving wheels: 2.045m (6ft 8.5in)
Axle load: 18,636kg (41,000lb)
Fuel: 5,000kg (11,000lb)
Grate area: 1.91m² (20.56sq ft)
Water: 13,630 litres (3,000 Imp gal/ 3,600 US gal)
Heating surface: 126m² (1,351sq ft)
Superheater: 20.1m² (216sq ft)
Steam pressure: 14.1kg/cm² (200psi)
Adhesive weight: 36,818kg (81,000lb)
Tractive force: 8,086kg (17,790lb)

Below: **City of Truro** *posing at* **Southampton Terminus**

During the early 1900s, the GWR made a leap ahead in locomotive building practice. This was especially noticeable in express locomotives, for which duty the single-driver was then still widely used. A fresh approach in passenger locomotive design had been seen already in the Duke class of 1895. This had been developed into the Bulldog class, and then appeared for express passenger duties as the Badminton and Atbara classes, with a final evolution to the City class in 1903.

The boilers on the City class were without domes, and had Belpaire fireboxes. They were the work of the GWR's new mechanical engineer, George Jackson Churchward. The boiler barrel was coned to meet the top of the Belpaire firebox, rather in the manner of the American wagon-top boiler.

Below: *the 4–4–0 Armstrong class was originally designed by William Dean in 1894. The locomotives were later rebuilt by Churchward in 1910, with the same cylinder and wheel specification as the City class*

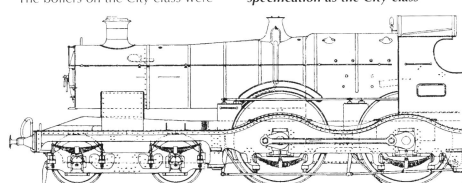

CLASS P8 4-6-0

Country of origin: Germany
Railway: Royal Prussian Union Railway (KPEV)
Date: 1906
Length overall: 18.592m (61ft)
Total weight: 78,409kg (172,500lb)
Cylinders: two 575 x 630mm (22.6 x 24.8in)
Driving wheels: 1.75m (5ft 9in)
Axle load: 17,727kg (39,000lb)
Fuel: 5,000kg (11,000lb)
Grate area: 2.58m² (27.8sq ft)
Water: 21,338 litres (4,700 Imp gal/ 5,700 US gal)
Heating surface: 143.3m² (1,542sq ft)
Superheater: 58.9m² (634sq ft)
Steam pressure: 12kg/cm² (170psi)
Adhesive weight: 51,818kg (114,000lb)
Tractive force: 12,140kg (26,760lb)

Right: originally Class P8 of the Prussian Railways

Below: Class P8 038.772 at Freudenstadt, July 1972

Since 1884 the KPEV had built both simple and compound locomotives, compounds predominating for express passenger work and simples for secondary passenger work. No fewer than 272 mixed-traffic Class P6 2-6-0s were built between 1903 and 1910, but their driving wheels did not produce the required speeds. An enlarged 4-6-0 design was introduced in 1906 but these locomotives proved to be unreliable and suffered from many breakdowns, which made them unpopular. The Class P8 was the result of experiments to find an improved 4-6-0, and was classified initially for secondary passenger and mixed

traffic work. The P8 went on to become the most widely-used and popular mixed-traffic steam engine ever to be built.

The mixed-traffic design was built from 1906; eventually no less than 3,956 were built. At the end of the First World War, many of the Class P8 were dispersed throughout Europe as a result of reparations. The P8 became an engine universally used in Germany for many years, becoming Class 38 first of the *Deutsche Reichsbahn* and later of the German Federal Railway, on which these locomotives ended their days.

A few were still running in eastern Europe into the 1980s.

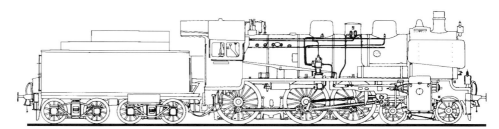

CARDEAN CLASS 4–6–0

Country of origin: UK
Railway: Caledonian Railway (CR)
Date: 1906
Length overall: 19.964m (65ft 6in)
Total weight: 133,636kg (294,000lb)
Cylinders: two 527 x 660mm (20.75 x 26in)
Driving wheels: 1.981m (6ft 6in)
Axle load: 18,863kg (41,500lb)
Fuel: 5,000kg (11,000lb)
Grate area: 2.4m² (26sq ft)
Water: 22,700 litres (5,000 Imp gal/ 6,000 US gal)
Heating surface: 168.5m² (1,814sq ft)
Superheater: 48m² (516sq ft)
Steam pressure: 14.1kg/cm² (200psi)
Adhesive weight: 55,909kg (123,000lb)
Tractive force: 10,282kg (22,667lb)

Originally CR No 903 Cardean, *this 4–6–0 was photographed at Garve in the early 1930s. It was renumbered 14752 and the name was removed on being painted in LMS colours*

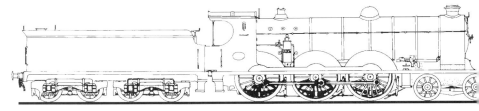

There were just five of these beautiful Cardean class 4–6–0s, all built at the Caledonian Railway's own St Rollox shops in 1906. Their design did not break any new ground, featuring as it did inside cylinders and motion with Stephenson's valve gear, which drove slide valves situated on top of the cylinders via rocking levers. Superheaters were added in 1911–2, and later still vacuum-brake equipment was fitted, so that the vacuum-braked trains of other companies could be handled.

The locomotives were allocated to one driver and to one train at a time. On every weekday one ran the famous western corridor with the 2pm from Glasgow to London, taking it as far as Carlisle. There it waited, to return in the evening with the corresponding train from London's Euston terminus. Such was the relationship between man and machine that the resultant degree of reliability was well beyond the reach of any other railway administration.

The Class 908 mixed-traffic 4–6–0, of which ten examples were built at the same time and also at St Rollox, was the mixed-traffic cousin of the Cardean.

Cardean was the last of the class to be withdrawn in 1930, at which time it was London, Midland & Scottish No 14752.

STAR CLASS 4-6-0

Country of origin: UK
Railway: Great Western Railway (GWR)
Date: 1907
Length overall: 19.56m (64ft 2in)
Total weight: 73,100kg (161,185 b)
Cylinders: four 381 x 660mm (15 x 26in)
Driving wheels: 2.05m (6ft 8.5in)
Axle load: not known
Fuel: not known
Grate area: 2.51m² (27sq ft)
Water: not known
Heating surface: 171.07m² (1,841sq ft)
Superheater: 24.4m² (263sq ft)
Steam pressure: 15.8kg/cm² (225psi)
Adhesive weight: 55,700kg (122,819lb)
Tractive force: 12,600kg (27,800lb)

A four-cylinder passenger 4-6-0 was put into production from 1906, as a result of the trials on the Great Western Railways (GWR) with the de Glehn four-cylinder compounds Nos 102, 103 and 104. The type was good for 145km/h (90mph), and in superheated form could haul trains of up to 559 tonnes (550 tons). In their time, these George Churchward-designed simple locomotives, the first of which was No 4001 *Dog Star*, were superior to any other 4-6-0 in Britain. They lasted in service until the withdrawal of No 4056 *Princess Margaret*, which had itself been built in 1910. They had inside Walschaert's valve gear and derived motion for the outside valves. Just as with the de Glehn compounds, the inside cylinders were connected to the first pair of driving wheels and those outside to the second pair.

The valves of the outside cylinders were driven by horizontal rocking levers connecting the back end of the inside valve spindle with the front end of the outside one. Each lever was bent backwards from the fulcrum to the outside valve spindle connection, to correct the valve events of the inside and outside cylinders for the angularity of their connecting rods.

Bottom: *No 4061 Glastonbury Abbey at Old Oak shed in 1955*

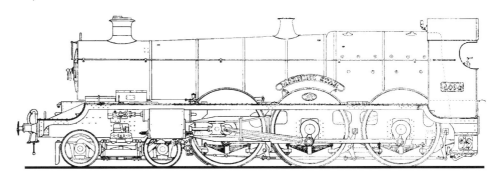

4500 CLASS 4–6–2

Country of origin: France
Railway: Paris-Orléans Railway (PO)
Date: 1907
Length overall: 20.79m (68ft 2.5in)
Total weight: 136,818kg (301,000lb)
Cylinders: two 420 x 650mm (16.5 x 25.6in) high-pressure; two 640 x 650mm (25.2 x 25.6in) low-pressure
Driving wheels: 1.9m (6ft 2.75in)
Axle load: 17,727kg (39,000lb)
Fuel: 6,136kg (13,500lb)
Grate area: 4.27m² (45sq ft)
Water: 19,976 litres (4,400 Imp gal/ 5,280 US gal)
Heating surface: 195m² (2,100sq ft)
Superheater: 63.5m² (684sq ft)
Steam pressure: 16kg/cm² (232psi)
Adhesive weight: 53.181kg (117,000lb)

Below: restored No 4546 on exhibition at the Musée Français du Chemin de Fer *(French National Railway Museum), Mulhouse*

Built by the *Société Alsacienne* for the PO, the 4500 class was the first Pacific to be run in Europe. It also became the most powerful and the most efficient 4–6–2 steam locomotive ever to be run in Europe. A round 100 were built between 1907 and 1910, together with a further 90 3500 class, which were built with 100mm (4in) smaller diameter wheels between 1909 and 1918. All were four-cylinder de Glehn compounds, and later examples were delivered superheated.

One interesting feature of the class was its trapezoidal grate, which was wide at the back but narrower in the front where it sat between the frames.

Although they were good engines, to begin with they were not outstanding until the arrival of André Chapelon. He proposed a rebuild of these locomotives and in 1929 a transformation was effected.

Chapelon achieved a 25% increase in power by pre-heating the feed water with waste heat from the exhaust and providing an additional heating surface in the firebox. He used a superheater which was 24% larger with larger steam pipes which improved steam flow, and switched to poppet valves which worked more quickly and provided bigger openings. He also improved the exhaust system to give greater draught with less back-pressure, by means of a double chimney. The overall result was complicated but nothing short of spectacular.

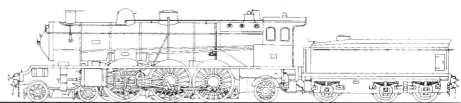

CLASS S 2–6–2

Country of origin: Russia
Railway: Ministry of Ways of Communications
Date: 1911
Length overall: 23.74m (77ft 10.5in)
Total weight: 168,000kg (370,500lb)
Cylinders: two 575 x 700mm (22.5 x 27.5in)
Driving wheels: 1.85m (6ft 0.75in)
Axle load: 18,000kg (39,600lb)
Fuel: 18,000kg (39,600lb)
Grate area: 4.72m² (51sq ft)
Water: 23,000 litres (5,000 Imp gal/ 6,000 US gal)
Heating surface: 198m² (2,131sq ft)
Superheater: 89m² (958sq ft)
Steam pressure: 13kg/cm² (185psi)
Adhesive weight: 54,000kg (118,800lb)
Tractive force: 13,653kg (30,092lb)

Right and below: the standard Russian passenger locomotive Class Su 2–6–2

A ministerial decree issued in March 1908, intended to ensure the replacement of old motive power, resulted directly in this 2–6–2 locomotive class. The first examples of Class S were built by the Sormovo works at Nijni Novgorod (now Gorky) in 1911, and by 1918 at least 900 of them were in use. The Class had a Krauss-Helmholtz truck at the front end and a bissel truck at the rear. Among the Class were a few built in 1913 for the standard gauge, rather than the Russian 1.52m (5ft) gauge. These worked on the railway from Warsaw to Vienna in what is now Poland, and were known as Class Sv.

Class S was an important passenger locomotive all over western Russia for more than 30 years, and a few were still working in the 1980s. Production lasted for a period of 40 years, and there was also an enlarged version, the Class Su, of which about 900 were built between 1926 and 1941.

Production continued after the Second World War, and concluded after a total of about 3,750 Class S locomotives had been built. Many of the locomotives were adapted for oil burning, and were used especially during the mid-nineteenth century on the Russian railways that were established in the vicinity of oilfields.

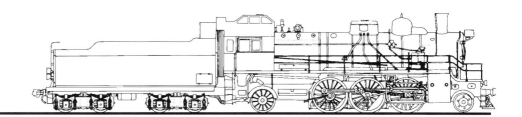

CLASS 231 C 4–6–2

Country of origin: France
Railway: Paris, Lyons & Méditerranée (PLM)
Date: 1912
Length overall: 20m (65ft 7in)
Total weight: 145,500kg (320,500lb)
Cylinders: two 440 x 650mm (17.3 x 25.6in) high-pressure; two 650 x 650 (25.6 x 25.6in) low-pressure
Driving wheels: 2m (6ft 6.7in)
Axle load: 18,500kg (40,500lb)
Fuel: 5,000kg (11,000lb)
Grate area: 4.3m² (45.7sq ft)
Water: 28,000 litres (6,160 Imp gal/7,400 US gal)
Heating surface: 203m² (2,185sq ft)
Superheater: 65m² (694sq ft)
Steam pressure: 16kg/cm² (228sq ft)
Adhesive weight: 55,000kg (122,000lb)

Right: the engineer in his cab of Class 231 H (third batch) No 720

Below: Class 231 K No 721 at Cherbourg, August 1964

The PLM railway produced two prototype 4–6–0 locomotives in 1909. One of these was simple, the other compound expansion. The compound engine enables a higher proportion of the steam energy to be converted into work during expansion, but this needs higher steam pressure which in turn causes higher boiler maintenance costs.

Trials were run in 1911 and the simple engine, which was superheated, developed higher power and used less coal than the compound one. As a result, 70 locomotives of the simple type were ordered, but the following year a batch of 20 was ordered for production as superheated compound types. These were followed by another batch of 70 simples. When comparisons were drawn between the two types of superheated engine, the compound was found to have a 25% lower coal consumption combined with a better performance. The railway stopped building the simples, and in due course converted its existing simples to compounds.

CLASS 231 D 4–6–2

Country of origin: France
Railway: État (State) railway
Date: 1914
Length overall: 22.97m (75ft 4.5in)
Total weight: 136,000kg (300,000lb)
Cylinders: two 420 x 650mm (16.5 x 25.6in) high pressure; two 640 x 650mm (25.25 x 25.6in) low pressure
Driving wheels: 1.95m (6ft 4.5in)
Axle load: 18,500kg (40,700lb)
Fuel: 6,000kg (13,500lb)
Grate area: 4.27m² (45sq ft)
Water: 20,000 litres (4,400 Imp gal/5,280 US gal)
Heating surface: 196m² (2,110sq ft)
Superheater: 80m² (861sq ft)
Steam pressure: 17kg/cm² (242psi)
Adhesive weight: 55,000kg (121,500lb)
Tractive force: not known

Class 231 D No 589, ahead of No 473

At the turn of the century the Ouest (Western) railway of France, with its restrictive loading gauge, was a shining example of how not to run a railway. Its bungling management decisions were clearly reflected in the locomotive design.

The railway was taken over by the State in 1908, and it would be only fair to say that the État's bureaucracy was itself no model of efficiency. From 1914 the new administration equipped the Ouest with express passenger locomotives of the Pacific type, based on those of the much more efficient Paris to Orléans line. This new class of locomotives differed from their Paris-Orléans forebears in that they had a round-topped firebox design in place of the Belpaire type.

After the First World War the government adopted the design as a French standard, and placed an order for 400 locomotives. Of these, 280 were delivered to the État lines, 100 to the Alsace-Lorraine railway, and others to the Est (Eastern), Nord (Northern) and Paris-Orléans (PO) railways.

Following the appointment of Raoul Dautry as its director in the late 1920s, the État finally became organised and embarked on a rebuilding programme based on Chapelon principles. The programme included upgrading 269 of the huge 4–6–2 fleet to have increased superheaters, double chimneys and larger passageways from 1928 onwards. Poppet valves were fitted on the LP side only of 134 of the Class 231D locomotives.

The results of the rebuilding were evident in the emergence of a class of excellent, robust and efficient locomotives. The class was quite capable of running over level ground at constant speeds of 100km/h (62mph) with either fast expresses or overloaded wartime trains, which often extended to 22 coaches frequently packed with 2,500 passengers.

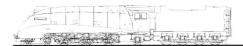

K4 CLASS 4–6–2

Country of origin: USA
Railway: Pennsylvania Railroad (PRR)
Date: 1914
Length overall: 25.451m (83ft 6in)
Total weight: 242,272kg (533,000lb)
Cylinders: two 686 x 711mm (27 x 28in)
Driving wheels: 2.032m (6ft 8in)
Axle load: 32,727kg (72,000lb)
Fuel: 16,363kg (36,000lb)
Grate area: 6.5m² (70sq ft)
Water: 45,400 litres (10,000 Imp gal/ 12,000 US gal)
Heating surface: 375m² (4,040sq ft)
Superheater: 88m² (943sq ft)
Steam pressure: 14.4kg/cm² (205psi)
Adhesive weight: 95,454kg (210,000lb)
Tractive force: 20,170kg (44,460lb)

Pennsylvania Railroad Company K4 class No 5354 takes on water. Most of the class were built at the railroad's own workshops at Altoona

The United States built many locomotives of the 4–6–2 Pacific type. Among the best were the Class J1s, built for the Wabash Railroad by the American Locomotive Co (Alco) and Baldwin, and the New York Central's Class K3 which was introduced in 1912. The most celebrated of all, however, was the Pennsylvania's K4 class.

The Pennsylvania was one of the very few North American lines to approach self-sufficiency, as it had a design staff, its own workshops, and even more importantly a testing plant at Altoona, where locomotives could be run up to full power and speed on rollers. The prototype K4, which appeared in 1914, was tested at Altoona and recorded an output of 2,424kW (3,250hp) at 75.6km/h

(47mph) with a steaming rate of 30.4 tonnes (29.9 tons) per hour. Its most efficient rate was found to be 15.4 tonnes (15.2 tons) per hour, with a boiler efficiency of 76%.

The K4s were derived from the Class E6 Atlantics, and proved to be one of the great successes of American locomotive building. In all 425 were built, 350 at Altoona and the remaining 75 by Baldwin; thanks to the soundness of their design, they remained in service for over 30 years They were two-cylinder superheated simples, with Walschaert's valve gear.

Until the coming of the duplex locomotives after the Second World War, K4 class locomotives handled all of the Pennsylvania's express passenger traffic outside of the electrified area.

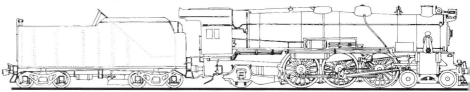

REMEMBRANCE CLASS 4–6–4T

Country of origin: UK
Railway: London Brighton & South Coast Railway (LBSCR)
Date: 1914
Length overall: 15.36m (50ft 4.75in)
Total weight: 101,000kg (222,000lb)
Cylinders: two 559 x 711m (22 x 28in)
Driving wheels: 2.057m (6ft 9in)
Axle load: 20,000kg (44,000lb)
Fuel: 3,500kg (8,000lb)
Grate area: 2.48m² (26.7sq ft)
Water: 12,000 litres (2,700 Imp gal/3,250 US gal)
Heating surface: 167.7m² (1,816sq ft)
Superheater: 35.6m² (383sq ft)
Steam pressure: 11.9kg/cm² (170psi)
Adhesive weight: 57,272kg (126,000lb)
Tractive force: 10,991kg (24,180 b)

Below: 4–6–4T No 333 (later 2333) Remembrance. This was the Southern Railway's War Memorial locomotive and bore these special plaques on the side tanks, below the nameplate, to that effect

This group of seven 4–6–4 tank locomotives was formed by the most powerful motive power steam engines ever to be owned by the London, Brighton & South Coast Railway (LBSCR). They were used as such on the renowned *Brighton Belle* trains, all-Pullman expresses that ran the distance of 82km (51 miles) between London Victoria and Brighton several times each day.

The Remembrance class locomotives were designed by Colonel L.B. Billinton. His instruction was to build a locomotive capable of reducing the journey time to 45–50 minutes. Despite the attainment of running speeds of up to 120km/h (75mph), this never happened. The journey time remained stubbornly at 60 minutes, and even when electric traction was introduced in 1933 could be only matched, not bettered.

The locomotives had outside Walschaert's valve gear, which actuated inside piston valves between the frames via rocking levers, but the cylinders were outside the frames.

The last of the class was built in 1922, when the company selected as a war memorial for those company employees who had given their lives during the First World War No 333, which was thus named *Remembrance*.

After electrification, the Southern Railway (SR) converted the 4–6–4 tanks into 4–6–0s, when they became known as Class N15X.

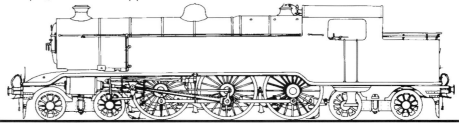

E1/D1 CLASS 4–4–0

Country of origin: UK
Railway: South Eastern & Chatham Railway (SECR)
Date: 1919
Length overall: 16.83m (55ft 2.75in)
Total weight: 93,000kg (204,000lb)
Cylinders: two 483 x 660mm (19 x 26in)
Driving wheels: 1.98m (6ft 6in)
Axle load: 17,500kg (38,000lb)
Fuel: 4,535kg (10,000lb)
Grate area: 2.2m² (24sq ft)
Water: 15,700 litres (3,450 Imp gal/ 4,143 US gal)
Heating surface: 119m² (1,276sq ft)
Superheater: 21m² (228sq ft)
Steam pressure: 12.7kg/cm² (180psi)
Adhesive weight: 34,000kg (75,000lb)
Tractive force: 8,170kg (17,950lb)

Below: *D1 class No 31505 at Kearsney, Kent, in September 1954*

After the end of the First World War, boat train traffic was switched from London's Charing Cross terminus to Victoria. This was not a problem in itself, but the railway lines that were in place formerly belonging to the London, Chatham & Dover Railway had severe weight restrictions. These precluded working on this route for the most powerful passenger locomotives of the South Eastern & Chatham (SECR), the L class 4–4–0s.

This weight problem was to be further compounded by the proposed introduction of better-quality corridor stock on the boat trains. No money was available to fulfil this plan, either for new locomotives or for new

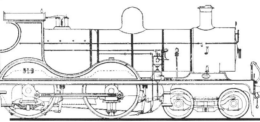

bridges, and the only course of action left open to locomotive superintendent Richard Maunsell was to upgrade some older locomotives.

To achieve this he took some aged 4–4–0 locomotives and gave them the Chapelon treatment. He produced a class of 32 small but handsome E1 class engines, which had larger grates and new fireboxes with the boiler centre line pitched 180mm (7in) higher to give greater depth to these new fireboxes. There were also piston valves with long-travel valve gear and larger superheaters.

The engines upgraded by Beyer, Peacock & Company were designated E1, and those upgraded by the railway company itself, D1. Although they were soon displaced by 4–6–0s on the prestigious boat trains, these locomotives performed outstandingly well on other routes as late as 1958.

Left: *a drawing of Class E, as it appeared originally in 1905 prior to upgrading to E1 class*

47xx CLASS 2–8–0

Country of origin: UK
Railway: Great Western Railway (GWR)
Date: 1919
Length overall: not known
Total weight: 83,490kg (183,680lb)
Cylinders: two 483 x 762mm (19 x 30in)
Driving wheels: 1.73m (5ft 8in)
Axle load: not known
Fuel: not known
Grate area: 2.82m² (30.28sq ft)
Water: not known
Heating surface: 208m² (2,232.1sq ft)
Superheater: 30m² (323.9sq ft)
Steam pressure: 15.8kg/cm² (225psi)

Britain's very first eight-coupled mixed-traffic engine was fitted with a larger boiler than those of Churchward's earlier locomotives, as a result of initial testing. The drive was on the second coupled axle, and

Below: No 4704 at Shrewsbury shed

the ratio of connecting rod to crank length was 5.5:1.

There was a tendency at about this time to slope the firebox roof downwards towards the back and also to slope the back plate outwards from the top to the foundation ring. This had been done on several railways, both for large Belpaire and for round-topped fireboxes, and had been copied from American practice.

The 47xx had outside cylinders, large driving wheels with a 6.1m (20ft) wheelbase and an overall wheelbase of 8.9m (29ft 3in). The steam pressure of 15.8kg/cm² (225psi) was the highest used for

mixed traffic, goods or mineral tender engine locomotives during the period between 1915 and 1925. Of the class's total heating surface of 208m² (2,232sq ft), 192m² (2,062sq ft) was provided by the tubes, and the balance of 16m² (170sq ft) by the firebox. This represents a higher percentage from the tubes than either Gresley's 2–8–0 that followed in 1921, or Raven's 0–8–0 of 1919, both of which also had smaller cylinders and smaller driving wheels.

Below: *Churchward's 2–8–0 at the time was the only eight-coupled mixed-traffic engine in the country*

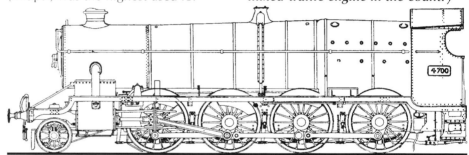

CLASS A1 4–6–2

Country of origin: UK
Railway: Great Northern Railway (GNR)
Date: 1922
Length overall: 21.46m (70ft 5in)
Total weight: 150,909kg (332,000lb)
Cylinders: three 508 x 660mm (20 x 26in)
Driving wheels: 2.032m (6ft 8in)
Axle load: 20,454kg (45,000lb)
Fuel: 8,181kg (18,000lb)
Grate area: 3.8m² (41.25sq ft)
Water: 22,700 litres (5,000 Imp gal/ 6,000 US gal)
Heating surface: 272m² (2,930sq ft)
Superheater: 49m² (525sq ft)
Steam pressure: 12.7kg/cm² (180psi)
Adhesive weight: 61,136kg (134,500lb)
Tractive force: 13,333kg (29,385lb)

The first British Pacifics to enter service were the aptly-designated A1s. They first took up their duties in April 1922, and eventually a total of 79 of these superb locomotives were built between 1921 and 1934.

Nigel Gresley had been appointed locomotive superintendent of the Great Northern Railway in 1911, and the A1s were his conception. They had three cylinders with one cylinder and one set of motion between the frames. These classic locomotives were not without their problems, especially their tendency for the large ends of the inside connecting rods to run hot, and damage to brakes through wheel burn when the A1s had started heavy trains from rest.

Alterations to the Walschaert's valve gear produced a considerable saving in coal; so much so, that the trains ran from London to Newcastle without a change of engine.

With boilers designed for a higher pressure of 15.75kg/cm² (225psi) and smaller cylinder diameters, these locomotives were designated A3 rather than A1, and sometimes referred to as Super Pacifics. The engine weight of these A3s was increased by 6.1 tonnes (6 tons) and their axle load by 2 tonnes (2 tons).

The longest non-stop journeys in the world were run by these A3 locomotives, over the 632km (392.75 miles) between London and Edinburgh during the summer months from 1928 onwards. The unstreamlined No 2750 *Papyrus* recorded a speed of 174km/h (108mph) near Peterborough in 1935, which remains as a world record for an unstreamlined steam locomotive.

No 2548 Galtee More *by the coaling plant at York, 1937*

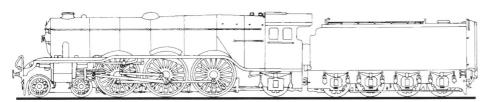

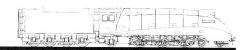

CASTLE CLASS 4–6–0

Country of origin: UK
Railway: Great Western Railway (GWR)
Date: 1923
Length overall: 19.683m (65ft 2in)
Total weight: 128,863kg (283,500lb)
Cylinders: four 406 x 660mm (16 x 26in)
Driving wheels: 2.045m (6ft 8.5in)
Axle load: 20,227kg (44,500lb)
Fuel: 6,136kg (13,500lb)
Grate area: 2.81m² (30.3sq ft)
Water: 18,160 litres (4,000 Imp gal/ 4,800 US gal)
Heating surface: 190m² (2,049sq ft)
Superheater: 24.4m² (263sq ft)
Steam pressure: 15.8kg/cm² (225psi)
Adhesive weight: 60,681kg (133,500lb)
Tractive force: 14,182kg (31,625lb)

Castle class No 5029 Nunney Castle, on the left of No 6024 King Edward I at Didcot in October 1994

By the time that the GWR had decided to replace the express Star class locomotives with something better, Charles Collett had succeeded Churchward as chief mechanical engineer. The former instructed his staff to work out the details of a Star enlarged to a 20.3 tonnes (20 tons) axle load. The resultant Castle class was pure Star, with the exception of the new No 8 boiler.

The first of the 154 Castle class locomotives went into traffic in August 1923, and at that time they were the most powerful locomotive design in the country, though far from being the largest. They were used to haul the *Cornish Riviera Limited* from London Paddington to Plymouth, at a scheduled speed of 88km/h (55mph)

for the 363km (225.7 miles). They also hauled the *Cheltenham Flyer*, which was for a time the fastest service in the world, with a 65-minute schedule for the 124km (77.25 miles) from Paddington to Swindon. On the same service in 1932 the *Tregenna Castle* accomplished an average speed for the journey of 131.5km/h (81.7mph) from start to stop, a world record which it retained for some time.

Withdrawal of these locomotives began in 1962, and the last Castle was retired from normal service in July 1965. No fewer than seven have been preserved, including *Caerphilly Castle* at the Science Museum in London as an example of the best in British locomotive engineering.

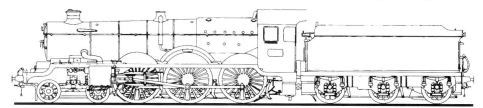

CLASS Ps-4 4–6–2

Country of origin: USA
Railway: Southern Railway (SR)
Date: 1923
Length overall: 28m (91ft 11.9in)
Total weight: 255,000kg (562,000lb)
Cylinders: two 686 x 711mm (27 x 28in)
Driving wheels: 1.85m (6ft 1in)
Axle load: 27,250kg (61,000lb)
Fuel: 14,545kg (32,000lb)
Grate area: 6.55m² (70.5sq ft)
Water: 53,000 litres (11,600 Imp gal/14,000 US gal)
Heating surface: 343m² (3,689sq ft)
Superheater: 92.3m² (993sq ft)
Steam pressure: 14.1kg/cm² (200psi)
Adhesive weight: 81,000kg (182,000lb)
Tractive force: 21,546kg (47,500lb)

The United States Railroad Administration (USRA), which took over the railroads for the duration of the First World War, had set out to establish a standard set of steam locomotive designs to cover all types of traffic, one of which was the USRA heavy 4–6–2. The Class Ps-4 was derived from a government-standard design, with the first 62 locomotives in the class being built by Alco in 1923 and 1926.

Southern Railway's President, Fairfax Harrison, replicated the English Southern Railway livery as nearly as possible, using a brighter green with gold lettering and line work, after visiting his company's namesake in the UK.

The second batch, which ran to 23 locomotives, were built in 1926 and had the 12-wheel tenders depicted below, which had a capacity of 16 tonnes (15.75 tons) of coal in addition to the 53,000 litres (11,600gal/14,000 US gal) of water.

The first batch had had only eight-wheel tenders. There was also a final batch of five locomotives, built by Baldwin.

The Class Ps-4 was the last steam passenger locomotive built for the Southern, remaining in prestige express duty until they were replaced by diesels. Their valve gear was either Walschaert's or Baker's, and three different types of feedwater heater were used: Coffin, Elesco or Worthington.

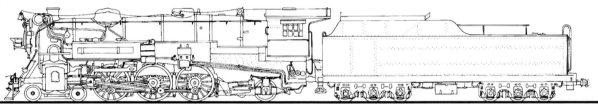

CLASS A 4–8–4

Country of origin: USA
Railway: Northern Pacific Railroad (NP)
Date: 1926
Length overall: 32.13m (105ft 4.4in)
Total weight: 335,000kg (739,000lb)
Cylinders: two 711 x 762mm (28 x 30in)
Driving wheels: 1.85m (6ft 1in)
Axle load: 29,500kg (65,000lb)
Fuel: 22,000kg (48,500lb)
Grate area: 10.7m² (115sq ft)
Water: 56,800 litres (12,500 Imp gal/15,000 US gal)
Heating surface: 433m² (4,660sq ft)
Superheater: 185m² (1,992sq ft)
Steam pressure: 15.8kg/cm² (225psi)
Adhesive weight: 118,000kg (260,000lb)
Tractive force: 27,950kg (61,600lb)

A number of different companies working for a variety of railways at last began producing the 4–8–4 in 1926. The first of over 40 North American railroads to use this wheel arrangement was the Northern Pacific, and hence the type name of Northern, used to describe a 4–8–4 locomotive.

The type was of great benefit to the Northern Pacific because its local coal reserves included a very high ash content and thus made necessary the use of a big firebox. The four-wheel truck at the rear enabled it to have a firebox of 4 x 2.5m (13.5 x 8.5ft).

Alco built the first 12 locomotives

The illustration below is of the final batch of A-5s, built in 1943 and distinguished by their 14-wheel tenders

of the class at Schenectady, but the rest of Northern's fleet of 4–8–4s was built by Baldwin in Philadelphia. The last batch all had the 14-wheel centipede or 4–10–0 tenders as in the drawing below, which were more usually associated with Union Pacific. They were designated A-5, a sub-class which appeared in 1943.

The A-5 was Northern's last steam order, and the locomotives were stretched to an overall length of 34.39m (112ft 10in), with a tractive force of 31,660kg (69,800lb) and an axle load of 33,650kg (74,000lb).

The Northern locomotives were used to haul the *North Coast Limited* running the 1,607km (999 miles) from St Paul to Livingston, Montana without a change of engine. On this route, however, they were probably burning a higher quality coal.

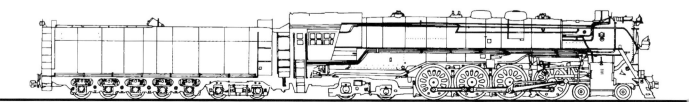

KING ARTHUR CLASS 4–6–0

Country of origin: UK
Railway: Southern Railway (SR)
Date: 1925
Length overall: 20.244m (66ft 5in)
Total weight: 141,136kg (310,500lb)
Cylinders: two 521 x 711m (20.5 x 28in)
Driving wheels: 2.007m (6ft 7in)
Axle load: 20,454kg (45,000lb)
Fuel: 5,000kg (11,000lb)
Grate area: 2.8m² (30sq ft)
Water: 22,700 litres (5,000 Imp gal/
6,000 US gal)
Heating surface: 174.5m² (1,878sq ft)
Superheater: 31.3m² (337sq ft)
Steam pressure: 14.1kg/cm² (200psi)
Adhesive weight: 61,136kg
(134,500lb)
Tractive force: 11,485kg (25,320 b)

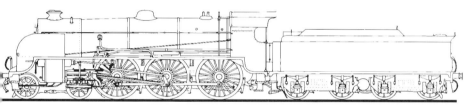

The new Southern Railway (SR), which had been formed by the amalgamation of the London & South Western (LSWR); the London, Brighton & South Coast (LBSC) and the South Eastern & Chatham Railways (SECR), appointed Richard Maunsell to the position of chief mechanical engineer. Immediately following this, he concentrated initially on improving his own SECR sector before turning his attention to the LSWR and its long-distance expresses which plied their trade between London and the West Country. These expresses took the shape of 4–6–0 N15 class locomotives in 1923, which although adequate were not outstanding.

Maunsell's new locomotive was an improved N15 with larger superheaters, more direct steam passages and improved combustion achieved by way of a redesigned ashpan. The first of the new class, No 453 *King Arthur*, was launched in early 1925 and was quickly followed by ten further engines.

Meanwhile, upgrading work was proceeding on 20 older locomotives to give them some of the new technical features, and these were soon followed by a further 30 new locomotives, which had been ordered from the North British Locomotive Company of Glasgow. A final 14 new 4–6–0 locomotives were built at the LSWR works at Eastleigh the following year. Although these had smaller 15,900-litre (3,500-gallon/ 4,200 US gal) six-wheel tenders than the first batch, they are included in the 74-strong King Arthur class.

The down Bournemouth at Winchester, hauled by No 739 King Leodegrance in 1938

CLASS 01 4–6–2

Country of origin: Germany
Railway: *Deutsche Reichsbahn* (DR)
Date: 1926
Length overall: 23.94m (78ft 6in)
Total weight: 109,090kg (240,000lb) excluding tender
Cylinders: two 600 x 660mm (23.5 x 26in)
Driving wheels: 2m (6ft 6.7in)
Axle load: 20,227kg (44,500lb)
Fuel: 10,000kg (22,000lb)
Grate area: 4.41m² (47.5sq ft)
Water: 34,050 litres (7,500 Imp gal/ 9,000 US gal)
Heating surface: 247.3m² (2,661sq ft)
Superheater: 85m² (915sq ft)
Steam pressure: 16kg/cm² (228psi)
Adhesive weight: 59,318kg (130,500lb)
Tractive force: 16,160kg (35,610lb)

With the formation of the *Deutsche Reichsbahn* on 1 April 1920, the new administration was faced with the problem of unifying more than 200 classes of locomotives, a quite unenviable task. It decided to establish an entirely new design standard, which would be introduced all over the country, and that as far as possible components and auxiliary apparatus should be interchangeable between classes.

Under the guidance of the engineer, Dr Richard P. Wagner, two new 4–6–2 express locomotive designs were initiated, both being introduced in 1925. One was a two-cylinder simple, the other being a four-cylinder compound, and they were designated Classes 01 and 02 respectively. Only ten of each were built at first, and after careful comparison the company concluded that the 02 compound did not show sufficient superiority over the Class 01 to justify its higher construction and maintenance costs, so that later on all of the Class 02 were rebuilt as 01s.

Although the basic layout of the 01 was simple, they were nonetheless complicated engines, with feedwater heaters, round-topped fireboxes that had almost straight fronts and boilers with parallel barrels. They were constructed with bar frames, and built by both Borsig of Berlin and AEG.

By 1938, a further 231 units had been built in addition to the ten 02 conversions, and 298 locomotives with an 18-tonne (17.7-ton) axle load, which were designated 03.

The DB (post-war West German) Class 01.008 at Bochum Dahlhausen, 1985.

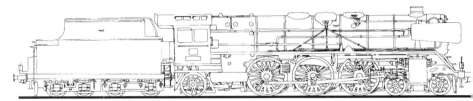

LORD NELSON CLASS 4–6–0

Country of origin: UK
Railway: Southern Railway (SR)
Date: 1926
Length overall: 21.297m (69ft 9.75in)
Total weight: 142,727kg (314,000lb)
Cylinders: four 419 x 610mm (16.5 x 24in)
Driving wheels: 2.007m (6ft 7in)
Axle load: 20,909kg (46,000lb)
Fuel: 5,000kg (11,000lb)
Grate area: 3.1m² (33sq ft)
Water: 22,700 litres (5,000 Imp gal/6,000 US gal)
Heating surface: 185m² (1,989sq ft)
Superheater: 35m² (376sq ft)
Steam pressure: 15.5kg/cm² (220psi)
Adhesive weight: 63,181kg (139,000lb)
Tractive force: 15,196kg (33,500lb)

The Lord Nelson class No 30854 Howard of Effingham, ex-works at Eastleigh, October 1951

There was a blaze of publicity for the unveiling of No 850 *Lord Nelson* in 1926. It was to be the prototype of a series of 16 locomotives, all of which were named after great seafarers.

The next seven locomotives in the class appeared in 1928, followed by eight in the following year. The class of beautiful 4–6–0s was introduced as a more powerful though more complex replacement for the hastily-prepared King Arthur class, and took over its duties on the heavy holiday expresses.

The Lord Nelsons had Belpaire fireboxes, large grates and interesting cranks which were set at 135 degrees to each other instead of the more usual 90 degrees. The overall effect was to give smoother running; the downside of this was that the coal in the tender was not shaken forward, and thus the firemen had to work harder the longer the journey lasted. Another of the firemen's complaints was that the class was hard to fire, a problem that was not solved for at least a decade, when eventually the air flow through the firegrate was improved by the fitting of a multiple-jet blast pipe arrangement, known as the Lemaître.

The disfavour these locomotives found with their crews was probably their downfall, because as there were so few of them experience of their working was not easily gained. The first of the class, *Lord Nelson*, has been preserved at the National Railway Museum, York.

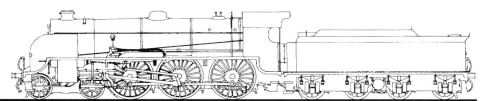

K3 CLASS 2–6–0

Country of origin: UK
Railway: London & North Eastern Railway (LNER)
Date: 1926
Length overall: 18.136m (59ft 6in)
Total weight: 73,700kg (162,500lb)
Cylinders: three 470 x 660mm (18.5 x 26in)
Driving wheels: 1.727m (5ft 8in)
Axle load: 20,300kg (44,750lb)
Grate area: 2.6m² (28sq ft)
Water: 19,000 litres (4,200 Imp gal/ 5,000 US gal)
Heating surface: 176.6m² (1,900sq ft)
Superheater: 37.81m² (407sq ft)
Steam pressure: 12.7kg/cm² (180psi)
Adhesive weight: 60,900kg (134,285lb)
Tractive force: 13,644kg (30,000lb)

Right: *the prototype three-cylinder K3 Mogul, built exclusively for general service on the LNER*

Below: *the K3 class No 61950 ex-works at Doncaster, May 1959*

During the second half of the 1920s, the most interesting trend in the gradual development of the general utility locomotive in Britain was represented by the London, Midland and Scottish (LMS) 2–6–0 of 1926 and by the Southern and Great Western 4–6–0s. Since the construction of the 43xx class of outside cylinder 2–6–0s on the Great Western Railway in 1911, the type had become very popular for fast goods and mixed-traffic duties. Prior to the grouping of the railways successful designs had been produced on the Great Northern; London, Brighton & South Coast; South Eastern & Chatham; Caledonian; and Glasgow & South Western Railways.

The Southern was becoming an increasingly frequent user by 1925, while on the London and North Eastern Railway (LNER) Sir Nigel Gresley was building his three-cylinder K3 class for duties on many parts of the system. Ten of Gresley's 2–6–0 H4 class had already gone into service in 1920, ahead of the 183 locomotives of his K3 class. The latter were a class of superheated three-cylinder simple machines with outside Walschaert's valve gear and derived motion for the piston valve of the inside cylinder. Gresley's derived motion was later to be a feature of many of his large three-cylinder designs.

The K3s were capable of hauling freight trains of up to 55 four-wheel wagons at 72km/h (45mph).

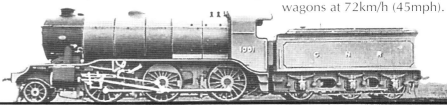

S15 CLASS 4–6–0

Country of origin: UK
Railway: Southern Railway (SR)
Date: 1927
Length overall: not known
Total weight: 137,565kg (303,744lb)
Cylinders: two 521 x 711m (20.5 x 28in)
Driving wheels: 1.702m (5ft 7in)
Axle load: 20,216kg (44,576lb)
Fuel: not known
Grate area: 2.6m² (28sq ft)
Water: 22,720 litres (5,000 Imp gal/ 6,000 US gal)
Heating surface: 174.5m² (1,878sq ft)
Superheater: 31.3m² (337sq ft)
Steam pressure: 14.1kg/cm² (200psi)
Adhesive weight: not known
Tractive force: 13,542kg (29,860 b)

Right: a Southern Railway Maunsell S15 class mixed traffic 4–6–0

Below: the S15 class No 30508 at Eastleigh shed, May 1957

The Southern Railway (SR) had become a large user of general utility locomotives by 1925, and the 4–6–0 type was becoming more favoured than the 2–6–0. The SR, following a practice that had been established by the London and South Western, had been building small-wheeled variants of the standard express passenger 4–6–0s but the H15 class of 1924, having 1.83m (6ft) diameter coupled wheels, seemed to lack the freedom in running necessary for a truly good utility machine.

The S15 class locomotives that followed them were a variant of Maunsell's King Arthur class express passenger engines, with the boiler pressure of his Lord Nelsons. They did very good work on the heavy fully-fitted night goods trains between London and Southampton, and between London and Exeter. The class was deployed essentially as goods rather than general-utility engines. The locomotives had been fitted with Maunsell superheaters, and the tenders which were capable of holding 22,720 litres (5,000 Imp gal/6,000 US gal) were double-bogied and each weighed 57.3 tonnes (56.4 tons).

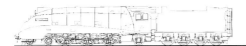

D49 CLASS 4–4–0

Country of origin: UK
Railway: London & North Eastern (LNER)
Date: 1927
Length overall: not known
Total weight: 116,114kg (256,032lb)
Cylinders: three 430 x 660mm (17 x 26in)
Driving wheels: 2.032m (6ft 8in)
Axle load: 21,315kg (47,600lb)
Fuel: not known
Grate area: 2.4m² (26sq ft)
Water: not known
Heating surface: 130m² (1,397.78sq ft)
Superheater: 25.25m² (271.8sq ft)
Steam pressure: 12.7kg/cm² (180psi)
Tractive force: 9,776kg (21,556lb)

Right: *an LNER three-cylinder 4–4–0 D49 class with piston valves and Westinghouse brakes, built at Darlington works in 1927*

Below: *No 62738* **The Zetland** *standing at Starbeck shed, May 1955*

Designed to perform intermediate duties in the north-eastern and Scottish areas of the London & North Eastern Railway (LNER), this class had the 4–4–0 wheel arrangement. The three-cylinder engines had a relatively high tractive effort, intended to take on the duties that had previously been worked by various classes of Atlantic and large 4–4–0s of North Eastern Railway (NER) and North British Railway (NBR) origin. These new Gresley locomotives had quite a few points of similarity to the Great Central Railway locomotives, particularly in the proportions of the boilers.

The earliest engines in the class were built at Darlington works in 1927, and had 203mm (8in) diameter piston valves actuated by Walschaert's gear and the Gresley conjugated motion in the middle cylinder. Later engines, built from 1932, had the rotary cam poppet valve gear.

Although capable of excellent work, these engines never fully superseded the Atlantics of the NER and NBR design, although in the hands of able and enthusiastic crews the piston-valve D49 4–4–0 did occasionally put up remarkably fine performances. The rotary cam poppet-valve engines were used mostly on NER services between Hull, Leeds, Scarborough and Newcastle.

CLASS XC 4–6–2

Country of origin: India
Railway: Indian Railways (IR)
Date: 1927
Length overall: 23.2m (76ft 1.5in)
Total weight: 178,000kg (392,500lb)
Cylinders: two 584 x 711mm (23 x 28in)
Driving wheels: 1.88m (6ft 2in)
Axle load: 19,750kg (43,500lb)
Fuel: 10,105kg (22,400lb)
Grate area: 4.75m² (51sq ft)
Water: 27,250 litres (6,000 Imp gal/ 7,200 US gal)
Heating surface: 226m² (2,429sq ft)
Superheater: 59m² (636sq ft)
Steam pressure: 12.7kg/cm² (180psi)
Adhesive weight: 59,500kg (130,000lb)
Tractive force: 13,895kg (30,625lb)

Three classes of 4–6–2 passenger engines were introduced in India after the First World War. Classified for light, medium and heavy work with axle loads of 13.2, 17.3 and 19.8 tonnes (13, 17 and 19.5 tons) respectively, they were known as Classes XA, XB and XC. Most of them were built by the Vulcan Foundry in Lancashire in England, and they were designed to burn poor quality coal.

Unfortunately the introduction was far from satisfactory; the locomotives were poor steamers and provided the most unpleasant of rides, so that the continual shuddering led to cracks in the boilers and fractures in the motion and frames. No fewer than 284 units had been built over an 11-year period before a fatal accident involving an XB in 1937 led to an investigation and ultimately to rectification of their inherent problems.

With Partition in 1947, some 60 of the Indian Railways' 4–6–2s went to Pakistan (now Bangladesh), leaving approximately 76 XAs, 81XBs and 50XCs in India. These were renumbered in 1957, by which time they had been relegated to minor duties. The last of these locomotives was withdrawn in 1981.

Below: *a standard gauge Class XC*
Bottom: *Class XB No 22169 at Charbagh works, November 1979*

89

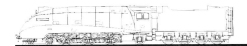

ROYAL SCOT CLASS 4–6–0

Country of origin: UK
Railway: London Midland & Scottish (LMS)
Date: 1927
Length overall: 19.787m (64ft 11in)
Total weight: 142,045kg (312,500lb)
Cylinders: three 457 x 660mm (18 x 26in)
Driving wheels: 2.057m (6ft 9in)
Axle load: 20,909kg (46,000lb)
Fuel: 9,090kg (20,000lb)
Grate area: 2.9m² (31.25sq ft)
Water: 18,160 litres (4,000 Imp gal/4,800 US gal)
Heating surface: 172m² (1,851sq ft)
Superheater: 34.1m² (367sq ft)
Steam pressure: 17.6kg/cm² (250psi)
Adhesive weight: 62,272kg (137,000lb)
Tractive force: 15,037kg (33,150lb)

After the grouping of the railways in the United Kingdom, the new London, Midland and Scottish Railway inherited over 5,000 locomotives. There was a great diversity of types, and many were old, so there was an urgent need to standardise on a fresh locomotive stock.

The North British Locomotive Company was commissioned to build a three-cylinder simple 4–6–0 express passenger class, and from 1927 the company very rapidly produced 50 of them. A further 20 locomotives were added to the class in 1930, but these were built at the old Midland Railway works in Derby.

These Royal Scots managed more than 30 years of top express work, although this period does cover an extensive rebuild programme, but they disappeared very quickly once dieselisation took hold. The first withdrawal was in October 1962, and the last in January 1966.

In their heyday, the Royal Scots could handle any express train in Britain. They had not only some power to spare but also ran more economically and just as ably as the bigger 4–6–2s. They had three cylinders, each with its own set of Walschaert's valve gear, and Belpaire fireboxes which were built to the maximum size that the loading gauge would permit.

Large smoke deflectors were fitted after 1931, following an accident at Leighton Buzzard where the smoke probably obscured the driver's view.

Bottom: *Locomotive No 6100* Royal Scot *at Crewe North shed, May 1939*

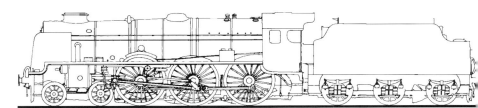

KING CLASS 4–6–0

Country of origin: UK
Railway: Great Western Railway (GWR)
Date: 1927
Length overall: 20.777m (68ft 2in)
Total weight: 138,181kg (304,000lb)
Cylinders: four 413 × 711mm (16.25 × 28in)
Driving wheels: 1.981m (6ft 6in)
Axle load: 22.954kg (50,500lb)
Fuel: 6,136kg (13,500lb)
Grate area: 3.19m² (34.3sq ft)
Water: 18,160 litres (4,000 Imp gal/ 4,800 US gal)
Heating surface: 204m² (2,201sq ft)
Superheater: 29m² (313sq ft)
Steam pressure: 17.6kg/cm² (250psi)
Adhesive weight: 68,636kg (151,000lb)
Tractive force: 18,285kg (40,300lb)

The most powerful of all the British 4–6–0 classes in terms of tractive force was the 30-strong King class of locomotives, built by the GWR in 1927. They were, in effect, a stretched Castle class locomotive, which itself had been a stretched Star class.

With four cylinders and a steam pressure of 17.6kg/cm² (250psi) they gave a tractive force of 18,285kg (40,300lb). They were fitted with GWR's No 8 boiler, but their weight restricted their route availability to the main lines to Bristol, Plymouth and Wolverhampton.

When the locomotives were first built they had a power output of 917kW (1,230hp), but after the fitting of a double chimney this was increased to 1,022kW (1,371hp). They retained the Belpaire firebox, the domeless tapered barrel boiler and had the inside cylinders driving the leading coupled axle, as had their ancestors. Walschaert's valve gear, also situated inside the frames, drove the valves of the inside cylinders.

The design of the bogie was unique, with outside bearings to the leading wheels and normal inside bearings to the trailing pair. A speed of 175km/h (108.5mph) was recorded by No 6015 *King Richard III* with the down *Cornish Riviera Limited* in September 1955.

Below: *a King class locomotive, cut away to show the inner workings, and* **bottom,** *preserved No 6024* **King Edward I** *at Didcot, October 1994*

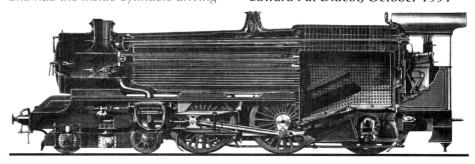

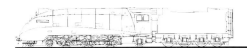

HALL CLASS 4–6–0

Country of origin: UK
Railway: Great Western Railway (GWR)
Date: 1928
Length overall: 11.25m (36ft 11in)
Total weight: 123,463kg (272,608lb)
Cylinders: two 470 x 762mm (18.5 x 30in)
Driving wheels: 1.83m (6ft)
Axle load: 19,250kg (42,448lb)
Fuel: 6,095kg (13,440lb)
Grate area: 291m² (27.07sq ft)
Water: 18,176 litres (4,000 Imp gal/ 4,800 US gal)
Heating surface: 170m² (1,831.38sq ft)
Superheater: 24.4m² (262.62sq ft)
Steam pressure: 15.8kg/cm² (225psi)
Tractive force: 12,370kg (27,275lb)

The Hall class locomotives were the standard mixed-traffic engine on the Great Western Railway (GWR). Production of the original Hall class proper began in 1928, and 259 were built to the 1928 design of Charles Collett. That class was equipped with two different types of tender although both held 18,176 litres (4,000 Imp gal/4,800 US gal) of water and about 6.1 tonnes (6 tons) of coal. One type had flat sides and was the last design of tender to be produced by the GWR.

These original Halls were the progenitors of the modern all-purpose 4–6–0 locomotive, and had been very easily developed from the standard two-cylinder 4–6–0s of the Saint class by the simple process of substituting 1.83m (6ft) for 2.03m (6ft 8in) coupled wheels. The prototype of the class was in fact a Saint, No 2925 *Saint Martin*, which was rebuilt in December 1924 for trial purposes.

The original Hall was modified during the early 1940s by F.W. Hawksworth, and 71 engines were built to the new design.

Externally the most noticeable differences were the extended frames, visible in front of the smokebox, and the longer steam pipe between the cylinders and the smokebox; but they also had a higher degree of superheat, as well as the famous Churchward standard No 1 boiler.

One of the original Halls, **Hinderton Hall,** *at Didcot in 1994*

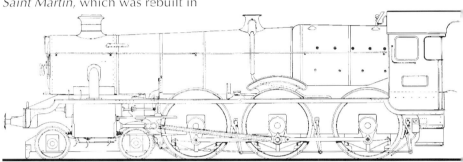

CLASS 6P (REBUILT PATRIOT) 4–6–0

Country of origin: UK
Railway: London Midland & Scottish Railway (LMS)
Date: 1930
Length overall: 19.73m (64ft 8.75in)
Total weight: 104,330kg (230,048lb)
Cylinders: three 430 x 660mm (17 x 26in)
Driving wheels: 2.057m (6ft 9in)
Fuel: 9,142kg (20,160lb)
Grate area: 2.9m² (31.25sq ft)
Water: 18,160 litres (4,000 Imp gal/ 4,800 US gal)
Heating surface: 173m² (1,862sq ft)
Superheater: 35.67m² (384sq ft)
Steam pressure: 17.6kg/cm² (250psi)
Tractive force: 13,583kg (29,950lb)

The original Patriot Class 5XP locomotives were rebuilt as the Class 6P and appeared as smaller versions of the Royal Scot, with all of the inherent strengths and weaknesses of that design. They were free-running and free-steaming under virtually all conditions, with excellent valve movements but, like the Scots, they had the Derby-type build-up smokebox which always caused trouble. Their Midland-inspired styling even made them appear similar to their forebears, but the Fowler tender created a more compact whole.

The first two examples were given two years of evaluation, during which period they established their superiority over the large-boilered Claughtons in terms of both efficiency and maintenance costs. The production run engines were built at Crewe and Derby between 1932 and 1934. The present class name did not appear until 1937, some three years after the old London and North Eastern Railway (LNER) war memorial engine *Patriot* had been withdrawn. That locomotive was never replaced by a three-cylinder 5XP, and so the first of its class, No 5500, was renamed from *Croxteth* to *Patriot*.

The locomotives performed well from the beginning, with few changes being made to them between building and scrapping. During the Second World War some engines received a coat of utility black but others survived in red, and after the War many received the full 1946 livery. During British Railways (BR) days 34 Patriots remained in un-rebuilt form, but all were eventually given BR lined green paint jobs.

They remained on main-line duty until the end, with the first example being withdrawn in September 1960.

Above: *LMS three-cylinder express passenger 4–6–0 Patriot class*
Below: *No 45517 at York shed, 1959*

SCHOOLS CLASS 4–4–0

Country of origin: UK
Railway: Southern Railway (SR)
Date: 1930
Length overall: 17.926m (58ft 9.75in)
Total weight: 111,591kg (245,800lb)
Cylinders: three 419 x 660mm (16.5 x 26in)
Driving wheels: 2.007m (6ft 7in)
Axle load: 21,363kg (47,000lb)
Fuel: 5,000kg (11,000lb)
Grate area: 2.63m² (28.3sq ft)
Water: 18,160 litres (4,000 Imp gal/ 4,800 US gal)
Heating surface: 164m² (1,766sq ft)
Superheater: 26.3m² (283sq ft)
Steam pressure: 15.46kg/cm² (220psi)
Adhesive weight: 42,727kg (94,000lb)
Tractive force: 11,400kg (25,133lb)

Right: *a line drawing of No 919 Harrow, which appeared in 1933*

Below: *Schools class No 30926 Repton, June 1962*

If the Lord Nelson class had disappointed, then the capabilities of the Schools class came as a pleasant surprise for the Southern Railway (SR). The Schools class was the second Southern 4–4–0 design, and on the basis of nominal tractive effort was the most powerful 4–4–0 ever to run in Europe. It was one of the most successful of all Maunsell designs, originating from a wish of the traffic manager for a locomotive of Lord Nelson characteristics but of intermediate power rating, and which would have a greater route availability than the 4–6–0 King Arthur class on which it was based.

The Schools design featured a shortened King Arthur boiler with a bigger ashpan, the result of a wide space between the coupled axles. The use of three cylinders with the drive on the leading coupled axle was intended to counter the boxing effect experienced on two-cylinder 4–4–0s. Walschaert's valve gear was used and the design as a whole proved a great success. A few locomotives were late fitted with multiple-jet blast pipes and larger-diameter chimneys.

The first of the class to appear was No 900, *Eton*, in 1930. This was followed by another nine examples, in a first batch that was built at Eastleigh. Another five appeared in 1932, ten in 1933, seven in 1934 and eight in 1935, bringing the total in class to 40 locomotives.

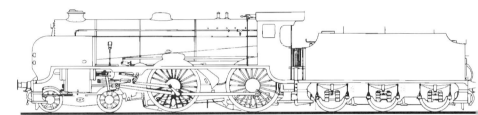

CLASS V 4–4–0

Country of origin: Ireland
Railway: Great Northern Railway (GNR[I])
Date: 1932
Length overall: 16.853m (55ft 3.5in)
Total weight: 105,454kg (232,000lb)
Cylinders: one 438 x 660mm (17.25 x 26in) high pressure; two 483 x 660mm (19 x 26in) low pressure
Driving wheels: 2.007m (6ft 7in)
Axle load: 21,363kg (47,000lb)
Fuel: 6,000kg (13,200lb)
Grate area: 2.3m² (25sq ft)

Water: 15,840 litres (3,500 Imp gal/ 4,200 US gal)
Heating surface: 116m² (1,251sq ft)
Superheater: 25.6m² (275sq ft)
Steam pressure: 17.6kg/cm² (250psi)
Adhesive weight: 41,818kg (92,000lb)

After the strengthening of the viaduct over the Boyne river in 1931, the use of a much more powerful engine became possible. Beyer, Peacock & Company of Manchester built the five Class V compounds, with the tenders being built at the Great Northern Railway's own Dundalk works. The locomotives were three-cylinder compounds, with three sets of Stephenson's link motion.

They ushered in a series of new and faster services, including a 54-minute Dublin to Dundalk schedule for the 138km (54.25-mile) distance. The Dublin to Belfast route, which included five stops and a Customs check, was newly scheduled for two hours and 28 minutes.

A second batch of five similar locomotives, classified as VS, was built in 1948. These had three simple cylinders, and Walschaert's valve gear.

Locomotive No 83 **Eagle** *at Adelaide shed, Belfast, May 1950*

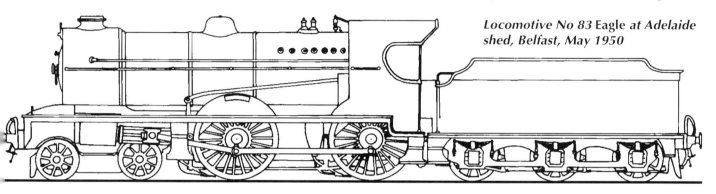

PRINCESS ROYAL CLASS 4–6–2

Country of origin: UK
Railway: London Midland & Scottish Railway (LMS)
Date: 1933
Length overall: 22.66m (74ft 4in)
Total weight: 106,400kg (234,100lb)
Cylinders: four 413 x 711mm (16.25 x 28in)
Driving wheels: 1.98m (6ft 6in)
Grate area: 4.27m² (45sq ft)
Heating surface: 252.04m² (2,713sq ft)
Superheater: 34.37m² (370sq ft)
Steam pressure: 17.5kg/cm² (250psi)
Adhesive weight:
68,000kg
(150,000lb)
Tractive force:
18,300kg
(40,300lb)

The first two four-cylinder simple 4–6–2s to be designed by William Stanier for the London, Midland and Scottish (LMS) made their appearance in 1933. Clearly it was Stanier's intention to rush into production with this new type, but only these two, Nos 6200 *The Princess Royal* and 6201 *Princess Elizabeth*, were built of three planned prototypes and they were not an instant success; in fact, they were a disappointment.

They had Walschaert's valve gear fitted for each cylinder, but following in the true Churchward tradition they had just 16 superheater tubes in what was a huge boiler. This, allied with the greater water circulation area, caused the steam-raising potential to be gained only at the cost of excessive coal consumption.

Stanier had a third boiler made with 32 superheater tubes, and fitted it to No 6200 in April 1935. The improvement was dramatic, and at last *The Princess Royal* began to show its true mettle. The main production batch of ten was then built with these revised superheater proportions.

*Below: Princess Victoria **as built in 1935, and** bottom, Princess Elizabeth **at Crewe works in 1938***

JUBILEE CLASS 5XP 4–6–0

Country of origin: UK
Railway: London Midland & Scotish (LMS)
Date: 1934
Length overall: 19.71m (64ft 8in)
Total weight: 81,000kg (178,300lb)
Cylinders: three 430 x 660mm (17 x 26in)
Driving wheels: 2.06m (6ft 9in)
Axle load: not known
Fuel: 9,143kg (20,160lb)
Grate area: 2.88m² (31sq ft)
Water: 18,176 litres (4,000 Imp gal/4,800 US gal)
Heating surface: 171m² (1,842sq ft)
Superheater: 2.85m² (31sq ft)
Steam pressure: 15.82kg/cm² (225psi)
Adhesive weight: not known
Tractive force: 12,100kg (26,600lb)

Locomotive No 45582 Central Provinces *on Bangor turntable, May 1957*

The first examples of the class came into service in 1934, immediately after the last of the Patriots had been completed, but they were disappointing.

They were derived from the parallel boiler engines but were difficult to fire because of inadequate draughting. Their erratic behaviour was a cause for consternation, considering that they shared their engine parts and boiler style with the successful Patriots and Stanier's two-cylinder Class 5P5F 4–6–0, which had entered service at the same time.

The Patriots had been rushed into production at the time of Stanier's arrival, and the Jubilee class was planned for volume production in much the same way, as the need for them was urgent. After considerable teething troubles, they were produced in two groups. These can be defined by their boiler proportions. The first series was given a short firebox and a domeless boiler with straight throatplate when new; the second series examples, from mid-1935, were built with sloping throatplates and domed boilers.

Built between 1934 and 1936, the class survived to become the final LMS express types in active BR service. The last example was withdrawn in 1967.

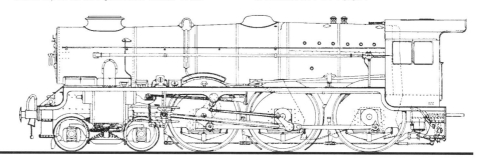

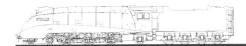

CLASS 5P5F 4–6–0

Country of origin: UK
Railway: London Midland & Scottish Railway (LMS)
Date: 1934
Length overall: 20.62m (67ft 7.75in)
Total weight: 129,000kg (285,000lb)
Cylinders: two 470 x 711mm (18.5 x 28in)
Driving wheels: 1.83m (6ft)
Axle load: 18,500kg (40,700lb)
Fuel: 9,000kg (20,200lb)
Grate area: 2.7m² (28.65sq ft)
Water: 18,160 litres (4,000 Imp gal/ 4,800 US gal)
Heating surface: 180m² (1,938sq ft)
Superheater: 28.5m² (307sq ft)
Steam pressure: 15.8kg/cm² (225psi)
Adhesive weight: 56,000kg (119,000lb)
Tractive force: 11,550kg (25,455lb)

Black Five No 45430 ex-works at Holyhead shed, September 1955

The famous Black Fives formed the most numerous and the most versatile class of steam locomotive in Great Britain. They had been intended to handle mixed traffic, but even the prototype was called in to haul London, Midland and Scottish (LMS) Railway's prestigious *Royal Scot* train. This weighed a massive 503 tonnes (495 tons) gross complete with 15 coaches, and yet the timing to Crewe was maintained. The Black Fives became the reliable deputies to both the 4–6–2 Princess Royal and 4–6–0 Royal Scot classes, and later they were allocated sheds on the Royal Scot route.

Designed by William Stanier, they were derived from the Hall class, and reflected the best practice from among the various areas of the LMS. They had Walschaert's valve gear and borrowed cylinders from the Lancashire & Yorkshire, boiler fittings from the Midland and their hooter-type whistle from the Caledonian. In total there were 842 Black Fives, produced over an 18-year period. They were built at the Crewe, Derby and Horwich workshops, at the Vulcan Foundry and at Armstrong-Whitworth.

They were the last British steam locomotives to haul timetabled express passenger trains.

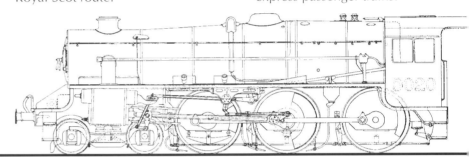

CLASS 8F 2–8–0

Country of origin: UK
Railway: London Midland & Scottish Railway (LMS)
Date: 1935
Length overall: 11.56m (37ft 11in) engine only
Total weight: 73,500kg (161,700lb)
Cylinders: two 470 x 711mm (18.5 x 28in)
Driving wheels: 1.42m (4ft 8in)
Axle load: 16,800kg (37,000lb)
Fuel: not known
Grate area: 2.6m² (27.8sq ft)
Water: 18,176 litres (4,000 Imp gal/ 4,800 US gal)
Heating surface: 176m² (1,895sq ft)
Steam pressure: 15.8kg/cm² (225psi)
Adhesive weight: 64,000kg (141,120lb)
Tractive force: 14,711kg (32,438lb)

Locomotive No 48532 passing Buxton Junction with a ballast train, in bright sunshine but after a little snow had fallen, February 1968

The LMS needed a new class of heavy freight locomotive in the early 1930s, to replace its ageing 0–8–0s which were of pre-Grouping design. However, it was not until the war years that production expanded to the point where the 8F eventually became the most numerous of the Stanier designs.

At the outbreak of war in 1939, preparations were made for the provision of rolling stock to support the army. The military strategists felt that it would be a long campaign, in the pattern of the First World War. The 8F 2–8–0 was the obvious choice to suit French conditions, and needed only a few slight modifications. However, by the time that the first locomotive of a batch of 230 was completed, the course of the War had altered and the Western Front had collapsed. Thus these Austerity 2–8–0s eventually took up service in the Middle East. A further batch of 90 which were equipped for oil burning were sent to Iran, while others were shipped to Egypt and Palestine and were used in the Western Desert campaign. The 8F was mainly built at Crewe and Horwich but further batches came from Ashford, Brighton, Darlington, Doncaster, Eastleigh and Swindon. The class finally numbered 736.

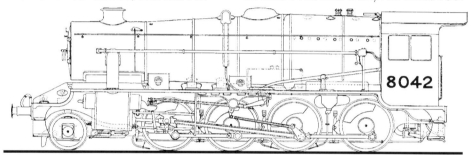

CORONATION CLASS 4–6–2

Country of origin: UK
Railway: London Midland & Scottish Railway (LMS)
Date: 1935
Length overall: 22.5m (73ft 10in)
Total weight: 110,000kg (242,990lb)
Cylinders: four 419 x 711mm (16.5 x 28in)
Driving wheels: 2.057m (6ft 9in)
Grate area: 4.65m² (50sq ft)
Heating surface: 260.67m² (2,806sq ft)
Superheater: 77.3m² (832sq ft)
Steam pressure: 17.5kg/cm² (250psi)
Adhesive weight: 68,600kg (151,263lb)
Tractive force: 18,140kg (40,000lb)

An experimental run by *Princess Royal* was an attempt to establish the feasibility of an average speed of over 96.5km/h (60mph) from London to Glasgow, while hauling a fair-sized load. As a result, Stanier embarked on his final class of Pacifics.

They were built between 1937 and 1948. While being of an almost sublime simplicity in pure y mechanical terms, they also benefitted from the experience gained with the Princess Royal class. It should be no surprise, therefore, that by the time production of the class ended, it was some three times greater in number than its predecessors.

Apart from the streamlining, the Coronations differed from their predecessors in several major respects. They had a much better and larger boiler with even more superheat; the driving wheels were 7.6mm (3in) larger, taking them to 2.06m (6ft 9in), for higher speed; the cylinder diameter was fractionally increased to maintain the 18,140kg (40,000lb) tractive effort; there were only two sets of valve gear; the inside valves were activated by rocking levers from the outside gear, and the outside cylinders were thus able to be moved to a more conventional position between the bogie wheels. Finally, the front-end steam circuit was much improved.

These locomotives formed the ultimate British passenger type built, as no British 4–6–2 ever exceeded the Stanier Coronations either in size or in performance capability. Whether streamlined or not, they were impressive machines that fulfilled their potential right from the outset.

Locomotive No 46256 **Sir William A. Stanier, F.R.S.** *in April 1962*

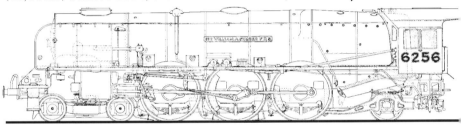

CLASS A4 4–6–2

Country of origin: UK
Railway: London & North Eastern Railway (LNER)
Date: 1935
Length overall: 21.64m (71ft)
Total weight: 167,795kg (370,000lb)
Cylinders: three 470 x 660mm (18.5 26in)
Driving wheels: 2.032m (6ft 8in)
Axle load: 22,448kg (49,500lb)
Fuel: 8,163kg (18,000lb)
Grate area: 3.8m² (41sq ft)
Water: 22,717 litres (5,000 Imp gal/6,000 US gal)
Heating surface: 240m² (2,576sq ft)
Superheater: 70m² (749sq ft)
Steam pressure: 17.5kg/cm² (250psi)
Adhesive weight: 67,118kg (148,000lb)
Tractive force: 16,086kg (35,455lb)

Preserved Class A4 No 60007 Sir Nigel Gresley in BR blue livery at Woodthorp in October 1994

Undoubtedly Britain's favourite locomotive, these 4–6–2 expresses hold the world's speed record for steam locomotives. This was attained by No 4468 *Mallard* at 202.7km/h (126mph), on a run recorded on 4 July 1938. The streamlined A4 was a direct descendant of the Class A1 4–6–2, and was planned to run the 429km (268 miles) between London and Newcastle in a scheduled four hours.

After Class A3 *Papyrus* was run with a six-coach train on the route in ten minutes under that time, the LNER decided to opt for a streamlined locomotive and train which was to be called the *Silver Jubilee*. In September 1935 the first of four Class A4 locomotives, No 2509

Silver Link, was fired up and on its press trip broke the British speed record three days before entering service.

A further 31 A4s were built. A few of them, including *Mallard*, were fitted with double blast pipes and chimneys. After the Second World War, in which one had been destroyed, they were renumbered from 1 to 34. Later still they became British Railways numbers 60001 to 60034, continuing to run all of the prestigious trains including the non-stop London to Edinburgh *Elizabethan*.

The last of the class to be withdrawn made its farewell in 1966, but six have been preserved including *Mallard*, which is at the National Railway Museum, York.

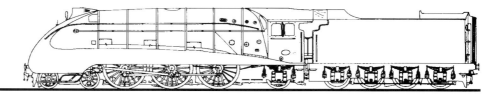

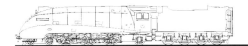

ANDES CLASS 2–8–0

Country of origin: Peru
Railway: Central Railway of Peru (FCC)
Date: 1935
Length overall: 18.88m (61ft 11.25in)
Total weight: 113,000kg (250,000lb)
Cylinders: two 508 x 711mm (20 x 28in)
Driving wheels: 1.32m (4ft 4in)
Axle load: 16,500kg (36,500lb)
Fuel: 6,656 litres (1,465 Imp gal/ 1,760 US gal)
Grate area: 2.6m² (28sq ft)
Water: 12,031 litres (2,650 Imp gal/ 3,180 US gal)
Heating surface: 160m² (1,717sq ft)
Superheater: 32m² (341sq ft)
Steam pressure: 14.1kg/cm² (200psi)
Adhesive weight: 66,000kg (146,000lb)
Tractive force: 16,600kg (36,600lb)

A short-boilered oil-fired Andes class 2–8–0 working the uncompromising Central Railway line

This class of 29 2–8–0s gave a very satisfactory performance on what is often regarded as the world's most demanding railway. The locomotives were built in small batches between 1935 and 1951.

They were also employed by the Central Railway's neighbours Southern Railway, which had 20 but with slightly larger driving wheels, and the Cerro de Pasco Railway which had five. The latter were the last five straight steam locomotives to be built by Beyer, Peacock & Company of Manchester.

The line of the Central Railway climbs from sea level to over 4,750m (15,750ft) within a distance of 150km (93 miles) from Lima to the high-altitude copper mines. Much of the climbing is done at gradients of up to 4% (one in 25), and thus for a steam locomotive to cope with this while negotiating double reversal bends to the summit is quite an achievement. The passengers were provided with oxygen, but nothing could be done about the lower temperatures at which the water boiled.

The engines had short boilers, narrow fireboxes and carried little water as there was ample available at the track side. Most importantly, they were fitted with air-sanding and later batches even carried a large box on the boiler top to carry the necessary quantity of sand required to complete the journey.

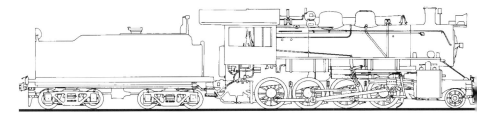

V2 CLASS 2–6–2

Country of origin: UK
Railway: London & North Eastern Railway (LNER)
Date: 1936
Length overall: 20.244m (66ft 5in)
Total weight: 146.818kg (323,000lb)
Cylinders: three 470 x 660mm (18.5 x 26in)
Driving wheels: 1.88m (6ft 2in)
Axle load: 22,500kg (49,500lb)
Fuel: 7,727kg (17,000lb)
Grate area: 3.86m² (41.25sq ft)
Water: 19,065 litres (4,200 Imp gal/5,040 US gal)
Heating surface: 225.8m² (2,431sq ft)
Superheater: 63.2m² (680sq ft)
Steam pressure: 15.5kg/cm² (220psi)
Adhesive weight: 66,364kg (146,000lb)
Tractive force: 15,304kg (33,730lb)

Although the 2–6–2 wheel arrangement, known as Prairie, originated in the midwest of the United States, the type was unable to find great favour there. In

consequence of this, the number built had barely topped the 1,000 mark by 1910. A single railroad, the Atchison, Topeka and Santa Fe, employed 235 of them, but even these were soon to be replaced by a combination of eight-coupled locomotives for freight and 4–6–2s for passenger work.

Perhaps the best-known and the best exponent of the 2–6–2 wheel arrangement was the V2 class of London and North Eastern Railway (LNER). These locomotives had been developed for express freight and the trains they hauled were called Green Arrows, for the insignia which

The famous No 4771 **Green Arrow** *at Sellafield, September 1974*

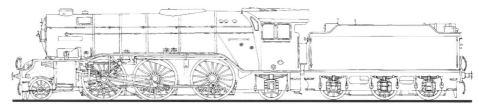

denoted express parcels that were guaranteed for next-day delivery.

They were remarkable locomotives, and the last class to be designed by Sir Nigel Gresley. By the time of the outbreak of the Second World War, there were already 86 examples of the class, which ultimately was to total 184.

Members of the class, of which only 11 carried names, achieved speeds of 149km/h (93mph) while running on the Yorkshire Pullman, and were at their best hauling the fast freights. During the war, they handled 25 packed coaches with consummate ease.

The last was withdrawn in 1966, and No 4771 *Green Arrow* has been preserved and is in working order.

CHALLENGER CLASS 4–6–6–4

Country of origin: USA
Railway: Northern Pacific Railroad (NP)
Date: 1936
Length overall: 37.16m (121ft 11in)
Total weight: 283,300kg (623,260lb)
Cylinders: four 584 x 813mm (23 x 32in)
Driving wheels: 1.753m (5ft 9in)
Axle load: 30,909kg (68,000lb)
Fuel: 22,000kg (48,400lb)
Grate area: 10m² (108sq ft)
Water: 70,300 litres (15,500 Imp gal/
18,600 US gal)
Heating surface: 431m² (4,624sq ft)
Superheater: 162m² (1,741sq ft)
Steam pressure: 17.5kg/cm² (250psi)
Adhesive weight: 193,200kg (425,000lb)
Tractive force: 47,400kg (104,200lb)

These were to all intents and
purposes the largest, heaviest,
strongest and most powerful steam
locomotives ever regularly to handle
express passenger trains. The type
was possible only because of its
articulation, and 47 examples were

built between 1936 and 1944 for the
NP with a further 65 for the Union
Pacific between 1942 and 1944.

Much work had gone into the
design, to produce Mallets that were
more stable when running in order to
enable them to attain higher speeds.
The Challengers were capable of
120kmh (74.25mph), and unlike the
Mallet compounds built previously
the Challengers were four-cylinder
simples. One of their design features
was the way in which the boiler was
carried on the frames to eliminate the
difficulties experienced with the
earlier Mallet compounds. These,
while running the front engine unit,
tended to be unloaded so that the
weight was thrown onto the rear
engine unit. Consequently, the front
unit tended to oscillate dangerously

at speed. In the Challengers, the
frame supports were so arranged that
more weight was transferred onto the
axles of the forward unit.

The locomotives were technically
sophisticated, with cast-iron frames,
roller bearing axle boxes, feed-water
heaters and disc driving wheels
without spokes. However, it was
found that they caused considerable
stress on the track, especially when
travelling at 100–120km/h (68–74.5
mph). The designers, however, held
that this was not because the class
was a Mallet design, but simply
because a locomotive of 300 tonnes
(295 tons) weight was being used at
these higher speeds for the first time.

Union Pacific Challenger class
No 3985 at Laramie, May 1983

CLASS GS-2 4–8–4

Country of origin: USA
Railway: Southern Pacific Railroad (SP)
Date: 1937
Length overall: 30.91m (101ft 5in)
Total weight: 401,364kg (883,000lb)
Cylinders: two 648 x 813mm (25.5 x 32in)
Driving wheels: 1.87m (6ft 1.5in)
Axle load: 31,330kg (68,925lb)
Fuel: 22,263 litres (4,900 Imp gal/ 5,900 US gal) oil
Grate area: 8.4m² (90.4sq ft)
Water: 88,984 litres (19,600 Imp gal/ 23,500 US gal)
Heating surface: 454m² (4,887sq ft)
Superheater: 194m² (2,086sq ft)
Steam pressure: 21.1kg/cm² (300psi)
Adhesive weight: 125,455kg (276,000lb)
Tractive force: 32,285kg (71,173lb)

Southern Pacific (SP) Railroad's *Daylight* was another harbinger of speed and comfort. These streamlined express locomotives hauled the famous train between Los Angeles and San Francisco, a distance of 756km (470 miles). Although the cars were described as lightweight, the 12-car train still amounted to 568 tonnes (559 tons), which was pulled at an average speed of 78km/h (48.5mph).

The original batch of these new 4–8–4s was designated GS-2, and had eight-coupled wheels and a grate area nearly 20% larger than the SP's then current GS-1 class of 4–8–4s. The newer locomotive had two cylinders and outside valve gear, and also sported three turbo-generators, a feed-water heater and a pump as well as injectors.

The GS-2s were introduced in 1937, and had 1.86m (6ft 1.5in) driving wheels. The GS-3s were little more than a second batch of GS-2s, and came in the same year, while the Class GS-4 of 1941 introduced fully enclosed cabs. Roller bearings were fitted to the GS-5s of 1942 and the final batch, classified GS-6 and introduced in 1943, had no streamlining. Their numbers all ran consecutively from the GS-2s, and were respectively 4410–15; 4416–29; 4430–57; 4458–9 and 4460–69.

Withdrawals began in 1954. The last to be withdrawn was No 4460 in October 1958, and this also brought SP steam operations to a close.

Below: *a Class GS-2 as delivered from the Lima Locomotive Works, Ohio, in 1937*

Bottom: *the GS-4 No 4449 at Sacramento, May 1981*

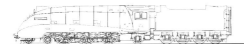

ROYAL HUDSON CLASS 4–6–4

Country of origin: Canada
Railway: Canadian Pacific Railway (CPR)
Date: 1937
Length overall: 27.686m (90ft 10in)
Total weight: 299,545kg (659,000lb)
Cylinders: two 559 x 762mm (22 x 30in)
Driving wheels: 1.905m (6ft 3in)
Axle load: 29,545kg (65,000lb)
Fuel: 21,364kg (47,000lb)
Grate area: 7.5m² (81sq ft)
Water: 54,480 litres (12,000 Imp gal/ 14,400 US gal)
Heating surface: 352m² (3,791sq ft)
Superheater: 143m² (1,542sq ft)
Steam pressure: 19.3kg/cm² (275psi)
Adhesive weight: 88,162kg (194,000lb)
Tractive force: 20,548kg (45,300lb)

Ex-Canadian Pacific Royal Hudson class No 2860, now preserved and running on the British Columbia Railway

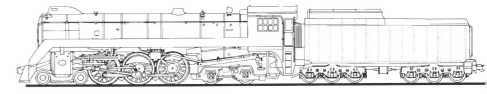

The Canadian Pacific Railway (CPR) had originally been incorporated by an Act of the British Parliament, and by 1930 was running Class G-3 4–6–2s as its top liners. In an attempt to improve upon the G-3s' performance, it created a series of 65 H-1 locomotives with fire grates that were 23% larger, and adopted a 4–6–4 wheel arrangement.

Their boilers had large superheaters and combustion chambers; there were arch tubes in the fireboxes and, as was becoming standard in North America for locomotives with larger grates, automatic stokers.

Once introduced, the H-1s reduced the number of engine changes from 14 to nine for the trans-Canada journey. For a time, the afternoon CPR *Royal York* train from Toronto to Montréal became the world's fastest scheduled train, an honour it lost to the Great Western (GWR) Railway's *Cheltenham Flyer*.

King George VI toured Canada in 1939, and for much of his visit home was a royal train. This was hauled by H-1 No 2850, which had been specially liveried in royal blue and silver with stainless steel boiler cladding. The royal arms were painted on the tender, and a replica crown was mounted on the running board. Similar crowns were later affixed to all of the CPR 4–6–4s which were built between 1937 and 1945.

CLASS 15F 4–8–2

Country of origin: South Africa
Railway: South African Railways (SAR)
Date: 1938
Length overall: 22.55m (74ft)
Total weight: 180,317kg (397,600lb)
Cylinders: two 610 x 711mm (24 x 28in)
Driving wheels: 1.52m (5ft)
Axle load: 19,000kg (42,000lb)
Fuel: 14,222kg (31,360lb)
Grate area: 4.49m² (48.3sq ft)
Water: 27,500 litres (6,050 Imp gal/ 7,250 US gal)
Heating surface: 257.8m² (2,775sq ft)
Superheater: 64m² (690sq ft)
Steam pressure: 14.8kg/cm² (210psi)
Adhesive weight: 73,700kg (162,508lb)
Tractive force: 21,800kg (48,000lb)

About 1,400 locomotives with the 4–8–2 wheel arrangement were built for SAR. These were the cumulative result of 26 major classes over a 42-year period. One of the most important, and certainly one of the most popular, was the Class 15 which had been introduced as the Class 15CA for the Cape Town to Johannesburg expresses as early as 1930, and had been built by the North British Locomotive Company. A variant of the class was the 15F, designed by W.A.J. Day and built just before the Second World War, although they were not produced in any quantity until after 1945.

The first locomotives of Class 15F

were built in Germany in 1938, seven by Schwartzkopf and another eleven by Henschel. They reverted to Walschaert's valve gear but included the important addition of roller bearings on the leading bogie, the trailing truck and also on the tender bogies. They also had mechanical stokers. A further 160 were built between 1945 and 1948 in Great Britain by Beyer, Peacock & Company and by North British. The class totalled 255 examples for the narrow 1.065m (3ft 6in) gauge.

SAR Class 15F No 3153 Melanie *with the Johannesburg to Mafeking Special at Derby, 1987*

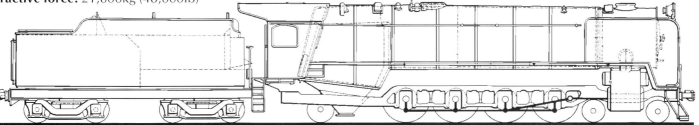

CLASS O 4–6–2

Country: Malaysia
Railway: Malayan Railway (PKTM)
Date: 1938
Length overall: 18.628m (61ft 1.4in)
Total weight: 102,727kg (226,000lb)
Cylinders: three 330 x 610mm (13 x 24in)
Driving wheels: 1.372m (4ft 6in)
Axle load: 12,982kg (28,560lb)
Fuel: 10,000kg (22,000lb)
Grate area: 2.5m² (27sq ft)
Water: 15,890 litres (3,500 Imp gal/ 4,200 US gal)
Heating surface: 103m² (1,109sq ft)
Superheater: 20.25m² (218sq ft)
Steam pressure: 17.5kg/cm² (250psi)
Adhesive weight: 39,091kg (86,000lb)
Tractive force: 10,859kg (23,940lb)

Right: *the 56 pre-war, as a Class O 4–6–2*

Below: *a Class 56 on the main West Coast line*

The Malayan Railway is comprised of just over 1,600km (1,000 miles) of metre-gauge (3ft 3.4in) track, and although it was running a fleet of 66 class 4–6–2s when dieselsation came in 1957, these disappeared very fast. In 1983 there was just a single steam locomotive left.

North British Locomotive Company of Glasgow was the supplier of these remarkable little engines, delivering 28 before and 40 after the Second World War.

The locomotives had the most beautiful balance, and were even tested at speeds of 112km/h (70mph) in an attempt to persuade the authorities to raise the prevailing speed limit of 72.5km/h (45mph). The limit remained unchanged, however,

and the 4–6–2s were left to supply in comfort what they were unable to deliver in scheduling; indeed, luxury travel was a feature of the *Golden Blowpipe* 'express'.

Great care was taken to reduce weight wherever possible, because of the axle weight restrictions. Bar frames were used and the boiler shell was of nickel steel. The inner firebox was also of steel, and the locomotives featured rotary-cam poppet-valve gear. They were originally designated Class 'O', with running numbers 60–87. However, after the War they were redesignated Class 56 and renumbered. They were all converted to burning oil instead of coal without detriment to their performance, before being withdrawn.

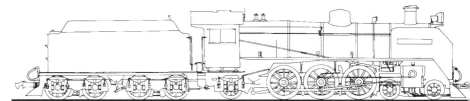

DUCHESS CLASS 4–6–2

Country of origin: UK
Railway: London, Midland & Scottish Railway (LMS)
Date: 1939
Length overall: 22.51m (73ft 10.25in)
Total weight: 164,545kg (362,000lb)
Cylinders: four 419 x 711mm (16.5 x 28in)
Driving wheels: 2.057m (6ft 9in)
Axle load: 23,864kg (52,500lb)
Fuel: 10,182kg (22,400lb)
Grate area: 4.6m² (50sq ft)
Water: 18,160 litres (4,000 Imp gal/ 4,800 US gal)
Heating surface: 261m² (2,807sq ft)
Superheater: 79.5m² (856sq ft)
Steam pressure: 17.6kg/cm² (250psi)
Adhesive weight: 67,045kg 147,500lb)
Tractive force: 18,144kg (40,000lb)

Locomotive No 6232 Duchess of Montrose *with no streamlining, no deflectors and a single chimney, on a Crewe local at Shrewsbury, 1938*

These were possibly the most powerful steam locomotives to run in Britain. The class name was given to ten locomotives built in 1938 that were similar to the streamlined Coronation class, save that for the second batch of five in the order no streamlined casing was provided. The first locomotive of the class was named *Duchess of Gloucester* and the rest were named after other Duchesses, with *Duchess of Buccleuch* being the first without the casing.

The unstreamlined locomotives caused much controversy. It is highly unlikely that the streamlining had any technical justification whatsoever; it was purely a fad of the era and a response to public taste. Although it is true to say that these locomotives looked superb in their streamlined casing, there are those who would contend that the Duchess was one of the handsomest classes to run in Great Britain even without it.

Each had a long boiler surmounting six large driving wheels, together with a bogie of 2.28m (7ft 6in) wheelbase to ensure good riding. Thus they provided excellent heavy cavalry for the general express passenger use on the west coast main line. They ran basically unchanged until being replaced by electric and diesel locomotives in 1964.

Three have been preserved, including No 6229 *Duchess of Hamilton*, which has been returned to main-line running order at York.

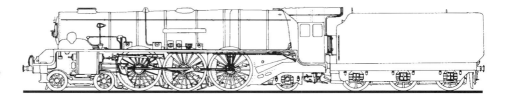

CLASS 12 4–4–2

Country of origin: Belgium
Railway: Belgian National Railways (SNCB)
Date: 1939
Length overall: 21.19m (69ft 6.25in)
Total weight: 85,682kg (188,500lb) excluding tender
Cylinders: two 480 x 720mm (18.8 x 28.4in)
Driving wheels: 2.1m (6ft 10.75in)
Axle load: 23,636kg (52,000lb)
Fuel: 7,955kg (17,500lb)
Grate area: 3.7m² (39.8sq ft)
Water: 23,971 litres (5,280 Imp gal/ 6,300 US gal)
Heating surface: 161m² (1,729sq ft)
Superheater: 63m² (678sq ft)
Steam pressure: 18kg/cm² (256psi)
Adhesive weight: 45,909kg (101,000lb)
Tractive force: 12,079kg (26,620lb)

A Class 12 No 12.004 streamlined locomotive at Louvain station, May 1978

These were utterly conventional as regards their principles, but were unusual if not unique in their layout. Belgium was still interested in high speeds, and these streamlined Class 12 locomotives were developed to operate light high-speed trains of three cars only and 160 tonnes (157.5 tons) over the 121km (71 miles) Bruxelles to Ostende route. The scheduled journey time was exactly one hour, including a four-minute halt at Bruges.

In operation they could accelerate from 0–140km/kh (87mph) within three minutes. The speed limit on the line was raised so that they could operate at this speed. While on trials, one had even recorded a speed of 165km/h (102.75mph), a fitting epitaph for the world's last 4–4–2. Coincidentally it was also the world's last inside-cylinder express steam locomotive.

The class featured a very wide firebox, and all six of them were built by the firm of Cockerill of Seraing, Belgium. Four examples had normal piston valves, but the other two featured Dabeg or Caprotti poppet valves.

As good as they were, these locomotives were able to operate for only a few months before the outbreak of the Second World War. One did survive hostilities, and is preserved at SNCB's locomotive depot at Louvain.

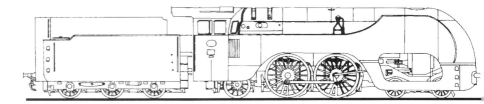

BIG BOY 4–8–8–4

Country of origin: USA
Railway: Union Pacific Railroad (UP)
Date: 1941
Length overall: 40.487m (132ft 10in)
Total weight: 540,682kg (1,189,500lb)
Cylinders: four 603 x 812mm (23.75 x 32in)
Driving wheels: 1.727m (5ft 8in)
Axle load: 30,795kg (67,750lb)
Fuel: 25,455kg (56,000lb)
Grate area: 13.9m² (150sq ft)
Water: 94,500 litres (20,800 Imp gal/ 25,000 US gal)
Heating surface: 547m² (5,889sq ft)
Superheater: 229m² (2,466sq ft)
Steam pressure: 21.1kg/cm² (300psi)

Adhesive weight: 245,455kg (540,000lb)
Tractive force: 61,422kg (135,375lb)

Although there were only 25, these were the ultimate in steam traction.

The Challenger class 4–6–6–4 Mallets had overcome the problem of weight distribution between the two sets of driving wheels, thus allowing higher operating speeds. They represented a very advanced machine that heralded the last step in the evolution of the steam locomotive.

However, many different railroads still competed with each other to acquire the best locomotives, and designs multiplied because each one was directed towards fulfilling ever

more specific needs. The climax of the Mallet type came when the Union Pacific Nos 4000–19 were built by the American Locomotive Company (Alco) in 1941, to be followed by another five in 1944.

A Mallet simple 4–8–8–4, this class was a development of the Challenger class of Northern Pacific. The Union Pacific class became known as the Big Boys because they were the largest, the most powerful and the heaviest locomotives that the world had ever seen or was to see, a fitting end to the epic drama of steam.

Union Pacific's Big Boy No 4016 gathers speed with a coal train

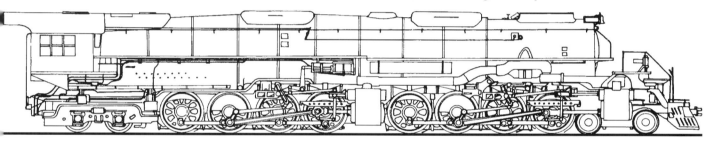

CLASS J 4–8–4

Country of origin: USA
Railway: Norfolk & Western Railway (N&W)
Date: 1941
Length overall: 30.759m (100ft 11in)
Total weight: 396,818kg (873,000lb)
Cylinders: two 686 x 813mm (27 x 32in)
Driving wheels: 1.778m (5ft 10in)
Axle load: 32,727kg (72,000lb)
Fuel: 31,818kg (70,000lb)
Grate area: 10m² (107.5sq ft)
Water: 75,818 litres (16,700 Imp gal/ 20,000 US gal)
Heating surface: 490m² (5,271sq ft)
Superheater: 202m² (2,177sq ft)
Steam pressure: 21kg/cm² (300psi)
Adhesive weight: 130,909kg (288,000lb)
Tractive force: 36,287kg (80,000lb)

The class was designed by Norfolk & Western (N&W), and built at its own Roanoke workshops to act as super locomotives for running express passenger trains.

They featured roller bearings to the axle boxes, mechanical lubricators servicing over 200 other bearings, Baker's valve gear and cast-steel frames. All but two of the class were streamlined.

Such was their high degree of maintenance and running condition and reliability that these remarkable engines covered 24,000km (15,000 miles) each month, yet they only visited the repair shops every 18 months. They could be fully serviced, greased, lubricated, cleaned of ash,

with their tenders replenished with coal and water in less than one hour, a truly impressive attribute. It is easy to see why N&W tried to hold on to its steam locomotives for as long as possible. They were the last steam locomotives to have been constructed in the United States, but they were retired in 1960.

They also handled, in addition to the N&W's own express trains, such trains on N&W lines as the original *Chattanooga Choo-Choo*s between Lynchburg and Bristol, on the famous journeys from New York to Chattanooga.

A Class J 4–8–4 of the N&W with a fast express passenger train in the Virginian hills

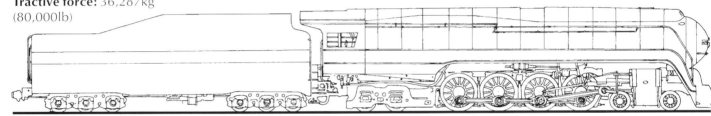

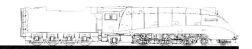

MERCHANT NAVY CLASS 4–6–2

Country of origin: UK
Railway: Southern Railway (SR)
Date: 1941
Length overall: 21.3m (69ft 10.5 n)
Total weight: 94,000kg (207,270lb)
Cylinders: three 457 x 610mm (18 x 24in)
Driving wheels: 1.88m (6ft 2in)
Axle load: 22,000kg (48,500lb)
Grate area: 4.5m² (48.5sq ft)
Water: not known
Heating surface: 227.7m² (2,450sq ft)
Superheater: 61.78m² (665sq ft)
Steam pressure: 19.6kg/cm² (280psi)
Adhesive weight: 64,000kg (141,120lb)
Tractive force: 17,000kg (37,500lb)

Merchant Navy class No 35024 East Asiatic Company *in standard blue livery with black and white lining at Waterloo, June 1949. The stock includes a Pullman car for the then Princess Elizabeth, who was visiting Weymouth*

Oliver Bulleid was appointed chief mechanical engineer of the Southern Railway in 1937. He went on to build a series of 4–6–2s, all with three cylinders and three sets of patent chain-driven valve gear inside an oil-filled sump between the frames.

He also used outside-admission piston-valves, driven from the centre via transverse oscillating shafts. The locomotives had big boilers and fireboxes that were tapered at the base line.

The first of the Bulleid 4–6–2s to appear were of the Merchant Navy class. The prototype was unveiled in 1941, and it was followed by a further 29 of the class. The West Country class was introduced in 1946, and benefitted from the experience gained in the running of the Merchant Navies.

The streamlined casing of the Merchant Navy class which incorporated the normal smoke deflector plates, was removed by British Railways between 1955 and 1959 to produce a handsome and powerful-looking locomotive in the traditional style. The weight of the class was greater than the original design weight, and like their West Country class siblings these locomotives were rebuilt with Walschaert's valve gear. They remained in service until 1967.

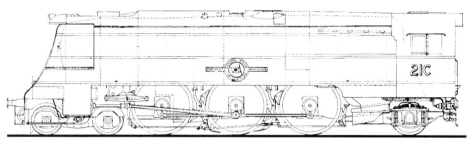

CLASS B1 4–6–0

Country of origin: UK
Railway: London & North Eastern Railway (LNER)
Date: 1942
Length overall: 11.32m (37ft 1.5in)
Total weight: 72,400kg (159,400lb)
Cylinders: two 508 x 660mm (20 x 26in)
Driving wheels: 1.88m (6ft 2in)
Fuel: 7,619kg (16,800lb)
Grate area: 2.5m² (27.5sq ft)
Water: 19,000 litres (4,200 Imp gal/5,000 US gal)
Heating surface: 186m² (2,005sq ft)
Steam pressure: 15.8kg/cm² (225psi)
Tractive force: 12,202kg (26,900lb)

The second most numerous class of 4–6–0 tender engines to be built in Britain was this Class B1 of the London and North Eastern Railway (LNER). First built in 1942 to replace a variety of 16 types of 4–6–0, 11 types of Atlantic and 48 types of 4–4–0, Class B1 amounted to 410 locomotives all delivered by 1950.

The Class B1 was built as a simple two-cylinder locomotive with outside cylinders and a synthesis of existing standard parts, and required a minimum of new machinery in order to produce it. Thus the boiler and the firebox were identical to those of the B17 or Sandringham class of three-cylinder express passenger 4–6–0s; the coupled wheels of 1.88m (6ft 2in) diameter were the same as those for the V2 and P2 classes, while the two cylinders with their steam chests were made from the patterns of the former Great Northern Railway (GNR) K2 2–6–0 which was then being maintained as a standard LNER class. The tender was the normal pattern for medium-powered locomotives.

Edward Thompson, who succeeded Sir Nigel Gresley in 1941, designed his locomotives with individual valve gear for each cylinder in order to eliminate the conjugated gear used by his predecessor. Although departing from the Gresley tradition of three-cylinder propulsion, the two cylinder B1 was a neat and compact looking locomotive.

Class B1 No 1134 sparkles with polished rods and full apple-green livery at Elgin, 1948

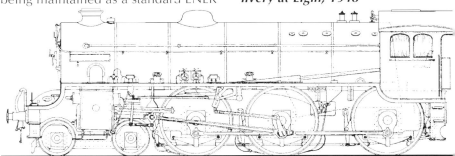

CLASS T1 4–4–4–4

Country of origin: USA
Railway: Pennsylvania Railroad (PRR)
Date: 1942
Length overall: 37.44m (122ft 10in)
Total weight: 433,500kg (954,000lb)
Cylinders: four 501 x 660mm (19.75
26in)
Driving wheels: 2.03m (6ft 8in)
Axle load: 31,500kg (69,000lb)
Fuel: 38,500kg (85,000lb)
Grate area: 8.5m² (92sq ft)
Water: 72,500 litres (16,000 Imp gal/
19,000 US gal)
Heating surface: 391m² (4,209sq ft)
Superheater: 131.9m² (1,430sq ft)
Steam pressure: 21.1kg/cm² (300psi)
Adhesive weight: 124,000kg (273,000lb)
Tractive force: 29,300kg (64,700lb)

During 1942, the Pennsylvania put
into service two prototypes of a new
4–4–4–4 express locomotive.
Although it was a four-cylinder
simple design, it was very complex,
particularly in its valve gear. It also

had two cylinders driving the front
pair of driving wheels while another
two cylinders drove the rear pair. The
streamlined casing of the locomotive
was designed by R. Loewy.

During road and test plant trials the
prototypes developed more than
4,900kW (6,580hp) at 137km/h
(85mph) but several design faults
were revealed that had to be
corrected before Class T1 could be
built in any quantity.

The company's own shops at
Altoona where the prototypes had
been built, together with the Baldwin
Locomotive Works, eventually built
another 50 of the class between 1945
and 1946.

The Class T1s could exceed 160km/h
(100mph) while heading passenger
trains of over 1,000 tonnes (984 tons)
and one was actually recorded at a
speed of 193km/h (120mph).

***Pennsylvania Railroad's 1940s
publicity brochure cover evokes the
atmosphere of the period***

CLASS Ul-f 4–8–2

Country of origin: Canada
Railway: Canadian National Railways
(CNR)
Date: 1944
Length overall: 28.496m (93ft 3in)
Total weight: 290,000kg (638,000lb)
Cylinders: two 610 x 762mm (24 x
30in)
Driving wheels: 1.854m (6ft 1in)
Axle load: 27,045kg (59,500lb)
Fuel: 18,182kg (40,000lb)
Grate area: 6.6m² (70.2sq ft)
Water: 52,210 litres (11,500 Imp gal/
13,800 US gal)
Heating surface: 333m² (3,584sq ft)
Superheater: 146m² (1,570sq ft)
Steam pressure: 18.3kg/cm² (260psi)
Adhesive weight: 107,727kg
(237,000lb)
Tractive force: 23,814kg (52,500lb)

The Canadian Ul series of eight-
coupled locomotives began in 1923,
with a batch of 16 built by the
Canadian Locomotive Company and

designated Ul-a. Then there followed the Ul-b in 1924, which comprised 21 locomotives, also built by the same company. Five further locomotives arrived in 1925 and were classified Ul-c, but this time they were built by Baldwin and used on CN's Grand Trunk Western subsidiary, which operated in the USA. The Ul-d and Ul-e classes followed in 1929 and 1930 respectively. The entire series had been numbered in sequence from 6000 to 6058.

Finally there came the batch of 20 Ul-f which had cast-steel frames, disc wheels, Vanderbilt cylindrical tenders and outside bearings on the leading bogies. More importantly, they also had exhaust steam injectors, which replaced the boiler feed pump and feed-water heater.

Some of the Ul-f engines were oil burners, but all were dressed up with side valences, British-styled flanged smokestacks, and green and black livery with brass numbers.

CLASS 141F 2-8-2

Country of origin: Spain
Railway: *Rede Nacional de los Ferrocarriles Españoles* (RENFE)
Date: 1944
Length overall: 25.5m (83ft 7.9in)
Total weight: 204,000kg (450,432 lb)
Cylinders: two 640 x 710mm (25.25 x 28in)
Driving wheels: 1.75m (5ft 9in)
Axle load: not known
Fuel: not known
Grate area: 5.3m² (57sq ft)
Water: not known
Heating surface: not known
Steam pressure: 16kg/cm² (228psi)
Adhesive weight: not known
Tractive force: 22,550kg (49,722lb)

Spain had introduced the 2–8–2 configuration in the 1920s, to cope with mountain gradients as well as lowland plains and for many years it was to form the basis of the Spanish main-line locomotive power. The nationalisation of the railways was an essential evolution of the system, primarily because of the poor condition of the rolling stock at the end of the Spanish Civil War (1936–9).

The first class to be built for RENFE after its formation in 1941 were the 57 locomotives of Class 141F, which were numbered from 2201 to 2257. The design was intended to meet the need for better motive power on the Madríd to Alicante line.

La Maquinista Terrestre y Maritima of Barcelona built two prototypes in 1944 and 1946, and thereafter another 55 locomotives were delivered between 1946 and 1952. They were also the most advanced of the 2–8–2 type to run in Spain. They had two cylinders and Lentz poppet valve gear was fitted, but they were not suited to high speeds. What they could do, however, was to haul almost any load demanded of them.

RENFE 141F No 2238 at Medina del Campo, August 1972

AUSTERITY CLASS 2–8–0

Country of origin: UK
Railway: War Department, Ministry of Defence (MOD)
Date: 1944
Length overall: 11.2m (36ft 9in)
Total weight: 71,400kg (157,080lb)
Cylinders: two 483 x 711mm (19 x 28in)
Driving wheels: 1.42m (4ft 8in)
Axle load: 15,847kg (34,944lb)
Grate area: 2.66m² (28.6sq ft)
Heating surface: 156m² (1,680sq ft)
Superheater: 28.8m² (310sq ft)
Steam pressure: 15.8kg/cm² (225psi)
Adhesive weight: 62,200kg (137,151lb)
Tractive force: 15,644kg (34,500lb)

These were by far the most numerous class of steam locomotives built in Britain. The North British Locomotive Company and the Vulcan Foundry between them constructed 935 examples in 1944, for use in Europe after the invasion.

They were based on the London, Midland and Scottish Railway (LMS)

Stanier Class 8F, but with Westinghouse braking substituted for the vacuum type. Cast iron was used in the normal way for the cylinders, for the blast pipe which was in one piece, and for the smokebox saddle which had the exhaust passages formed in it. The front end cylinder covers were of cast iron, and so was the chimney. Cast iron was also used in the manufacture of certain of the wheels, to replace steel. They were capable of handling loads of 1,016 tonnes (1,000 tons), at speeds of

about 66km/h (41mph) on level track.

A batch of 90 was sent to the Iranian State Railways and equipped for oil-firing, while others were used in Egypt, Palestine and in the Western Desert campaigns.

After the Second World War, 733 were returned to operate under British Railways Nos 9000–90732. All were withdrawn between 1959 and 1967, when they were destroyed.

R.A. Riddles' Austerity 2–8–0s as built by North British, below, *and* bottom, *No 90041 under steam, with a full tender*

AUSTERITY CLASS 2–10–0

Country of origin: UK
Railway: War Department, MOD
Date: 1944
Length overall: 12.57m (41ft 3in)
Total weight: 79,700kg (175,400lb)
Cylinders: two 480 x 710mm (19 x 28in)
Driving wheels: 1.43m (4ft 8.5in)
Axle load: 13,700kg (30,240lb)
Grate area: 3.7m² (40sq ft)
Heating surface: 181m² (1,951sq ft)
Superheater: 39.3m² (423sq ft)
Steam pressure: 15.8kg/cm² (225psi)
Adhesive weight: 68,200kg (150,381lb)
Tractive force: 15,530kg (34,200lb)

The former 8F freight locomotive of London, Midland and Scottish Railway (LMS) was redesigned in 1942 for further production. The intention in doing so was to have some locomotives to supply to Europe after its liberation from the Nazi régime. In addition to that 2–8–0 Austerity locomotive, there were also 150 of the 2–10–0 type, all built by North British, with enlarged boilers and firegrates for the purpose of burning low-grade fuel.

Members of this class proved to be very competent locomotives, and comparative tests carried out with a dynamometer car after the Second World War showed clearly their advantage in general performance over the earlier 2–8–0 design. This arose from the combination of the large boiler and wide firebox of the 2–10–0.

Of the 150 built, 25 were returned to Britain for use by British Railways. All were withdrawn in 1961.

Below: R.A. Riddles (left) and A. Black in front of a 2–10–0

Bottom: *No 90773 at Grangemouth shed, June 1962*

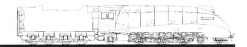

FEF-3 CLASS 4-8-4

Country of origin: USA
Railway: Union Pacific Railroad (UP)
Date: 1944
Length overall: 34.696m (113ft 10in)
Total weight: 412,727kg (908,000lb)
Cylinders: two 635 x 813mm (25 x 32in)
Driving wheels: 2.032m (6ft 8in)
Axle load: 30,455kg (67,000lb)
Fuel: 22,727kg (50,000lb)
Grate area: 9.3m² (100sq ft)
Water: 89,052 litres (19,600 Imp gal/23,500 US gal)
Heating surface: 393m² (4,225sq ft)
Superheater: 130m² (1,400sq ft)
Steam pressure: 21kg/cm² (300psi)
Adhesive weight: 121,136kg (266,500lb)
Tractive force: 28,950kg (63,800lb)

Below: the last batch of UP FEF class locomotives were all converted to oil burning soon after entering service. They were eventually withdrawn in 1959; FEF-3 locomotive No 8444 at Denver, July 1982

The last steam train to be built for the Union Pacific (UP) was the FEF-3 No 844, and this was also the locomotive that in 1958 hauled the *City of Los Angeles* over the last stretch of the train's journey of 232km (145 miles) on the leg from Grand Island into Omaha.

The class had its origins in the late 1930s, when the loads had begun to become too much for the 4–8–2s and a Class 700 hauling UP President William Jeffers' business car broke down. That did start things moving, and in 1938 Alco delivered 20 of the 4–8–4s.

The first batch was designated FEF (for four-eight-four)-1, and numbered from 800. The following year, 15 further examples with larger wheels and cylinders were delivered, designated FEF-2s. A final batch of ten locomotives, identical to the second batch, came in 1944, and the specification for them is detailed here. These were to be the last of UP's steam.

141R (LIBERATION) CLASS 2-8-2

Country of origin: France
Railway: Société National des Chemins de Fer (SNCF)
Date: 1945
Length overall: 26.161m (79ft 3in)
Total weight: 18,809kg (413,800lb)
Cylinders: two 596 x 711mm (23.5 x 28in)
Driving wheels: 1.65m (5ft 5in)
Axle load: 22,050kg (48,510lb)
Fuel: 10,909kg (24,000lb)
Grate area: 5.2m² (55.5sq ft)
Water: 1,468 litres (6,666 Imp gal/8,000 US gal)
Heating surface: 251m² (2.699sq ft)
Superheater: 65m² (704sq ft)
Steam pressure: 15.4kg/cm² (220psi)
Adhesive weight: 80,182kg (176,400lb)
Tractive force: 20,191kg (44,500lb)

By 1945 the SNCF was desperately short of locomotives to work the war-torn railways of France. Part of its immediate requirements were met at

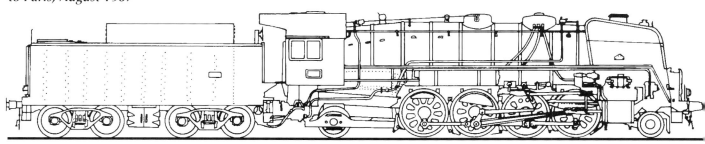

an average of 100 locomotives each week. This supply was maintained by three US and two Canadian builders; Baldwin Locomotive Works, Alco, Lima, Montréal Locomotive Works and Canadian Locomotive Works respectively. The construction of the first 700 locomotives started in January 1945, and the first was delivered on 30 July 1945. A total volume of 20,000 tonnes (19,685 tons) of engines and spares had to be transported over nearly 6,000km (3,729 miles). Various types of ships

Below: *SNCF 141R (Liberation)*
No 86 on the 15.31 from Boulogne
to Paris, August 1967

were used from the American and Norwegian merchant fleets. Liberty ships and cargo ships took part in the operation. The class was built to Imperial dimensions between August 1945 and July 1947, with a well-proportioned boiler with $316m^2$ (3,400sq ft) of heating surface. The 2–8–2 type was to find widespread use all over the French railway system and 1,340 examples were built before July 1947.

These were among the last steam locomotives to work on the SNCF. One of the 141R class, also known unofficially as the Liberation class, often substituted on the boat trains to

Calais after the withdrawal of the Pacifics from that duty. The type was not fast, but one of them could haul a sleeping car of 800 tonnes (787.4 tons) at over 100km/h (62mph) or 1,500 tonnes (1,476.4 tons) of freight at 50km/h (31mph). Passenger trains on steeply-graded routes were also within their capabilities and so they were used also along the French Riviera, between Marseilles and Ventimiglia.

Another often-forgotten advantage of the 141Rs was the ability of non-professional crews to handle them, which was an important factor in Europe after the Second World War.

COUNTY CLASS 4–6–0

Country of origin: UK
Railway: Great Western Railway (GWR)
Date: 1945
Length overall: 11.58m (37ft 11.75in)
Total weight: 59,733kg (131,712lb)
Cylinders: two 470 x 762mm (18.5 x 30in)
Driving wheels: 1.90m (6ft 3in)
Axle load: 19,700kg (43,456lb)
Grate area: 2.68m² (28.84sq ft)
Water: 18,176 litres (4,000 Imp gal/ 4,800 US gal)
Heating surface: 159m² (1,714sq ft)
Superheater: 24.6m² (265sq ft)
Steam pressure: 19.69kg/cm² (280psi)
Tractive force: 14,775kg (32,580lb)

The only new class to appear on the GWR in the last years before nationalisation was the County class two-cylinder 4–6–0 of 1945. This might have seemed a curious series of departures from the precepts of Swindon works in that non-standard features were introduced without there

being an obvious reason for them.

These locomotives were not notably successful in traffic in their early days, but now can be regarded retrospectively as guinea pigs. After Charles Collett had retired in 1941, the Second World War precluded building a new design intended purely for high-class express passenger service. However, Collett's successor, F.W. Hawksworth, had been considering post-war express passenger locomotive development. Towards the end of the War authorisation was given for further 4–6–0 mixed traffic engines, and this

provided the opportunity to try out a boiler of 19.69kg/cm² (280psi). Hawksworth intended to use the Castle boiler, suitably modified, and so without any appreciable tooling the 19.69kg/cm² (280psi) boiler was produced, of a weight suitable for the new mixed-traffic 4–6–0. Thus emerged the County class, which was further distinguished by the double blast pipe and chimney which appeared on the first of class, No 1000 *County of Middlesex*.

The Shrewsbury to Plymouth train hauled by No 1025 County of Radnor, *May 1955*

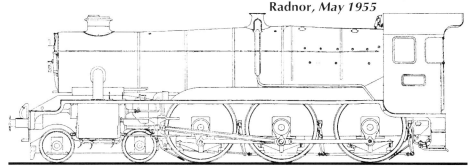

WEST COUNTRY CLASS 4–6–2

Country of origin: UK
Railway: Southern Railway (SR)
Date: 1946
Length overall: 20.542m (67ft 4.75in)
Total weight: 138,182kg (304,000lb)
Cylinders: three 416 x 610mm (16.7 x 24in)
Driving wheels: 1.879m (6ft 2in)
Axle load: 22,227kg (44,500lb)
Fuel: 5,000kg (11,000lb)
Grate area: 3.55m² (38.25sq ft)
Water: 24,790 litres (5,500 Imp gal/ 6,600 US gal)
Heating surface: 197m² (2,122sq ft)
Superheater: 50.6m² (545sq ft)
Steam pressure: 19.7kg/cm² (280psi)
Adhesive weight: 59,545kg (131,000lb)
Tractive force: 14,083kg (31,046lb)

West Country class No 34107 Blandford Forum ex-works at Weymouth shed, June 1963

These were smaller locomotives than Bulleid's 4–6–2 Merchant Navy class which immediately preceded them. The first 48 of the class had names associated with locations in the west country. These were followed by a further 70 locomotives, including what is now regarded as the Battle of Britain class. There is no technical distinction between the two classes.

Their features included an 'air-smoothed' casing, disc-type wheels with holes rather than spokes to reduce their weight and the type of multiple-jet blast pipe which became known as the Lemaître. They had also rocker grates, steam power-operated fire-hole doors and reversers, and electric lights which all benefitted the crew. Later models were also fitted with a system for reducing the scale that built up in the boilers, known as *traitement intégral Armand* (TIA).

Between 1957 and 1960, 60 West Country class locomotives were rebuilt with new conventional cylinders and motion, which made the class undoubtedly one of the very best ever to run in the UK. They achieved some outstanding feats of weight haulage at high speed and in the closing days of steam they worked the prestigious *Brighton Belle* on numerous occasions. The last steam train into Waterloo was the up Weymouth boat express in July 1967, headed by West Country class No 35030 *Elder Dempster Lines*.

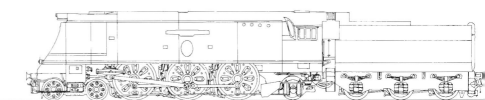

CLASS 561xx 2–10–0

Country of origin: Turkey
Railway: Turkish State Railways
Date: 1946
Cylinders: two 650 x 660mm (25.625 x 26in)
Driving wheels: 1.45m (4ft 9.125in)
Grate area: 3.98m² (43sq ft)
Heating surface: 239m² (2,575sq ft)
Superheater: 84.4m² (908sq ft)
Steam pressure: 16kg/cm² (228psi)
Tractive force: 26,104kg (57,560lb)

Many of these 2–10–0s were built by Beyer, Peacock & Company for mixed traffic on the Turkish State Railways. They were a development of a German design which had previously been built by a number of manufacturers, but while the outline of the design and the arrangement of cab fittings followed the practice previously favoured in Turkey, British methods of construction incorporated many proprietary fittings.

The engines were built on bar frames 89mm (3.5in) thick, with fully compensating suspension. Both air and automatic Westinghouse brake equipment were included, together with the Riggenbach counter-pressure brake apparatus for use in descending low grades with the engine in reverse.

At the beginning of the 1980s the majority of locomotives on the State's 1.435m (4ft 8.5in) gauge 8,193km (5,092-mile) system were still steam and numbered in excess of 500.

Below: *a Turkish State Railways Class 561xx 2–10–0, as built by Beyer, Peacock & Co in 1946*

Bottom: *Turkish State Railways No 56332 at Caycuma, in April 1944*

CLASS WP 4–6–2

Country of origin: India
Railway: Indian Railways (IR)
Date: 1946
Total weight: 172,500kg (380,000lb)
Cylinders: two 514 x 711mm (20.25 x 28in)
Driving wheels: 1.7m (5ft 7in)
Axle load: 20,700kg (45,500lb)
Fuel: 15,000kg (33,000lb)
Grate area: 4.27m² (45sq ft)
Water: 27,250 litres (6,000 Imp gal/ 7,200 US gal)
Heating surface: 286.3m² (2,257sq ft)
Superheater: 67m² (725sq ft)
Steam pressure: 14.7kg/cm² (210psi)
Adhesive weight: 55,000kg (121,500lb)
Tractive force: 13,884kg (30,600lb)

This 4–6–2 was the fastest and most powerful steam locomotive class on the 1.676m (5ft 6in) gauge Indian Railways, and 40 years after its introduction there were still a great many examples working hard. India no longer runs steam trains regularly.

The first of the class was built in the United States by Baldwin, which also built 16 prototypes. These prototypes were designated Class WP/P and delivered to the then East India Railway in 1947, but many more have been built since. It is claimed that some 755 were built between 1947 and 1967. The locomotives are modern two-cylinder Pacifics with decorative semi-streamlining, faired

smokebox doors and enclosed cabs.

The IR had introduced Pacific locomotives in 1928 with three types XA, XB and XC, all of which had been built in Britain. A total of 284 had been supplied by 1938, but problems with the side-control on the bogies had led to several accidents, in one of which over 100 people were killed. The problem was overcome, and resulting from that a new specification was introduced, leading to the WP class of Pacifics.

Below: *Class XB intermediate Pacific, built by North British in 1928, and bottom, Class WP No 7672, Bangalore, March 1968*

CLASS 4F 2–6–0

Country of origin: UK
Railway: London, Midland & Scottish Railway (LMS)
Date: 1947
Length overall: 17.04m (55ft 11in)
Total weight: 77,155kg (170,128lb)
Cylinders: two 445 x 660mm (17.5 x 26in)
Driving wheels: 1.6m (5ft 3in)
Fuel: 4,063kg (8,960lb)
Grate area: 2.15m² (23sq ft)
Water: 15,840 litres (3,500 Imp gal/ 4,200 US gal)
Heating surface: 113m² (1,221sq ft)
Superheater: 21.46m² (231sq ft)
Steam pressure: 15.8kg/cm² (225psi)
Tractive force: 10,962kg (24,172lb)

Wartime conditions convinced the LMS that a more modern 4F was needed, especially as maintenance was becoming overwhelmingly expensive. Lower running costs with easier, shorter repair times in the sheds were necessary.

Thus although these locomotives were a well-overdue replacement for the Class 4F 0–6–0, they were greeted with some astonishment. Many observers granted them the dubious accolade of being the ugliest locomotives ever to grace the tracks of the British Isles.

The new 4Fs were strictly utilitarian: plate frames were retained on the basis that there was more space between them for a narrow firebox; there were two outside cylinders with Walschaert's valve gear; fabricated components were used wherever possible; pipework

was exposed and high running boards were fixed only to the boiler, so as to reduce strains.

Eventually smaller tender wheels were used, which alleviated the need for wheel arches in the bottom of the tender, and exterior water sieves were fitted for easier maintenance. They were essentially unorthodox-looking engines, exacerbated by their large double chimneys.

Bottom: *No 43063 and No 43000, tender-to-tender on the* Wansbeck Piper *near Woodburn, October 1961*

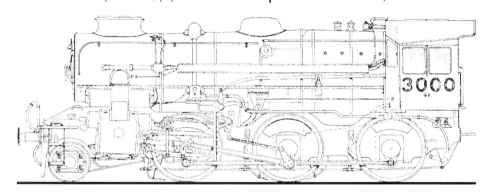

CLASS A1 4–6–2

Country of origin: UK
Railway: British Railways (BR)
Date: 1948
Length overall: 22.25m (73ft)
Total weight: 167,727kg (369,000lb)
Cylinders: three 482 x 660mm (19 x 26in)
Driving wheels: 2.032m (6ft 8in)
Axle load: 22,500kg (49,500lb)
Fuel: 9,091kg (20,000lb)
Grate area: 4.6m² (50sq ft)
Water: 22,700 litres (5,000 Imp gal/ 6,000 US gal)
Heating surface: 228.6m² (2,461sq ft)
Superheater: 63.2m² (680sq ft)
Steam pressure: 17.6kg/cm² (250psi)
Adhesive weight: 67,273kg (148,000lb)
Tractive force: 16,900kg (37,400lb)

A1 No 60130 Kestrel, *in post-war standard apple-green livery, couples to its train; photographed at King's Cross in 1961*

Sir Nigel Gresley died in 1941, and was succeeded as chief mechanical engineer of the London & North Eastern Railway by Edward Thompson, who inherited some 115 Pacifics and 600 other three-cylinder engines.

In his post-war building programme, Thompson planned to eliminate the troublesome derived motion used by Gresley. He wanted to replace it in the large engines with a third valve gear and in the smaller ones by discarding the third cylinder.

The first new locomotives were 15 Pacifics with 1.88m (6ft 2in) driving wheels, and these were classified as A2. They had a much more compact appearance than the rebuilds which had preceded them.

This class was followed by an order for a further 49 examples, but having 2.03m (6ft 8in) driving wheels. These were classified A1, and were not built until after nationalisation of the railways in 1948. They all had Kylchap (Kylala-Chapelon) double blast pipes, and five of them had roller bearings to all axles.

They proved to be both fast and economical, and handled much of the east coast express passenger work, with the exception of the King's Cross to Edinburgh non-stop trains.

They hold the distinction of achieving the highest daily mileage averaged over a 12-year period for any BR steam locomotive at 325km (202 miles), with the five that had the roller bearings managing 367km (228 miles) each day.

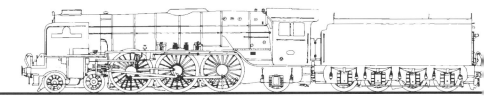

CLASS 241P 4–8–2

Country of origin: France
Railway: *Société National des Chemins de Fer* (SNCF)
Date: 1948
Length overall: 27.418m (89ft 11in)
Total weight: 214,545kg (472,000lb)
Cylinders: two 446 x 650mm (17.6 x 25.6in) high pressure; two 674 x 700mm (26.5 x 27.6in) low pressure
Driving wheels: 2.01m (6ft 7.1in)
Axle load: 20,455kg (45,000lb)
Fuel: 10,000kg (22,000lb)
Grate area: 5.1m² (54.4sq ft)
Water: 33,959 litres (7,480 Imp gal/8,980 US gal)
Heating surface: 244.6m² (2,633sq ft)
Superheater: 108m² (1,163sq ft)
Steam pressure: 20kg/cm² (284psi)
Adhesive weight: 82,227kg (180,900lb)

The last of the French-built Mountain classes was a batch of 35 engines, constructed by Schneider at Le Creusot in 1948. It was intended for use on the Dijon to Marseilles line before its electrification, and on trains from Paris to Lille and to Belgium.

Each locomotive had two high-pressure and two low-pressure cylinders as well as a large firegrate, made possible by a trailing axle. As with other French Mountain-type engines, however, they suffered from frame weakness; the frames were of only 28mm (1.1in) steel. This, combined with the double cranked axle, led to the campaign by Chapelon for the adoption of the

Below: *Chapelon's 241P Mountain, of which thirty-five examples were built, and* **bottom,** *No 29 departs Lille for Paris, shortly before the line was converted to electric traction in June 1958*

three-cylinder system for the national railways' more powerful 4–8–4 engine.

The Class 241P was built at the expense of France's last 40 2–8–2s, that were already on order. As time was a deciding factor, the locomotives were modifications of earlier Paris, Lyons & Méditerranée (PLM) 1930 designs and inevitably therefore a compromise. The result, not unnaturally, was that their mechanical performance left somewhat to be desired. Even so, by the time that deliveries were underway, electrification was also well advanced. The class did manage an active life of about 20 years, however, most of which was spent on the western region running out of Le Mans.

CLASS 24 2–8–4

Country of origin: South Africa
Railway: South African Railways (SAR)
Date: 1949
Cylinders: two 482 x 660mm (19 x 26in)
Driving wheels: 1.3m (4ft 3in)
Axle load: 9,650kg (21,280lb)
Fuel: 9,142kg (20,160lb)
Grate area: 3.34m² (36sq ft)
Water: 20,448 litres (4,500 Imp gal/ 5,400 US gal)
Heating surface: 152m² (1,641sq ft)
Superheater: 35.3m² (380sq ft)
Steam pressure: 14.1kg/cm² (200psi)
Tractive force: 14,186kg (31,280lb)

Right: *the SAR Class 24 2–8–4 locomotives were suitable for lines where the maximum permissible axle load was only 11.18 tonnes (11 tons)*

Bottom: *an SAR Class 24 No 3652 double-headed with Class 19D No 3324, at Toorwater with the* Sunset Limited *special train, April 1979*

This class of medium-powered locomotives was built for the 1.067m (3ft 6in) gauge railway of SAR, and was derived from the 1948 River class 2–8–2s of the Nigerian Railways. Two other designs, also allied to the River class, followed after the Class 24 in subsequent years. They were the Benguela Railways 4–8–2 of 1951, and the East African Railways 2–8–2 of 1952. All four designs were very similar.

The South African engine was suitable for lines where the maximum axle load was 11.2 tonnes (11 tons). A one piece cast-steel bed frame was used for the first time in any British-built locomotive. These were nearly 12.19m (40ft) long, and weighed about 10.2 tonnes (10 tons) each.

The SAR first tried the Vanderbilt tender tank on the main line Class 19D 4–8–2s. A few months later it adopted these tenders for the introduction of the 2–8–4 engines of Class 24. The 19D engines were very similar in outward appearance to the Class 24, except that they were generally larger and had bar frames. The tenders of both the Class 24 and the 19D engines were carried on six-wheeled bogies.

LASS YP 4–6–2

ountry of origin: India
ailway: Indian Railways (IR)
ate: 1949
ength overall: 19.088m (62ft 7.5in)
otal weight: 99,318kg (218,500lb)
ylinders: two 387 x 610mm (15.25 24in)
riving wheels: 1.372m (4ft 6in)
xle load: 10,682kg (23,500lb)
uel: 9,773kg (21,500lb)
rate area: 2.6m² (28sq ft)
Vater: 13,620 litres (3,000 Imp gal/ ,600 US gal)
eating surface: 103m² (1,112sq ft)
uperheater: 31m² (331sq ft)
team pressure: 14.8kg/cm² (210psi)

Adhesive weight: 31,364kg (69,000lb)
Tractive force: 8,731kg (18,450lb)

These were India's last express steam passenger locomotives to be built, between 1949 and 1970. They were all scaled for the metre gauge (3ft 3.4in), which at the time comprised about half of India's rail network; essentially they may be considered as being two-thirds full-size models of a standard US 4–6–2 Pacific.

Baldwin had supplied ten 4–6–2s to the state of Jodhpur in 1948, and so impressed was its railway administration that it approached Baldwin to supply 20 prototypes for a

Class YP. This was intended to be similar to the 1948 4–6–2s but slightly larger, although the tenders had a mere eight wheels rather than twelve.

Actual production orders were divided between 200 to come from Krauss-Maffei, and 100 to come from North British Locomotive Company, all 300 of which were to be delivered over a five-year period. The class eventually ran to 871 units, the remainder all being built by the Tata Engineering and Locomotion Company of Jamshedpur, India.

Class YP No 2372 departs from Madurai with a passenger train for Virundagar

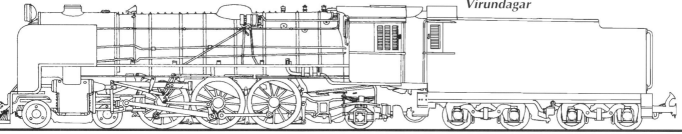

CLASS WG 2–8–2

Country of origin: India
Railway: Indian Railways (IR)
Date: 1951
Length overall: not known
Total weight: 98,900kg (217,300lb)
Cylinders: two 556 x 710mm (21.875 x 28in)
Driving wheels: 1.56m (5ft 1.5in)
Axle load: not known
Fuel: not known
Grate area: 4.27m² (45sq ft)
Water: not known
Heating surface: 277m² (2,982sq ft)
Superheater: 63.45m² (683sq ft)
Steam pressure: 14.8kg/cm² (210psi)
Adhesive weight: not known
Tractive force: 17,637kg (38,890lb)

Indian Railways purchased some 2–8–2 locomotives from the USA from 1943 onwards. A specification based on these engines was drawn up for a later version, known as the Class WG.

They used the same boiler dimensions as the WP passenger Pacifics, and the first 100 units were all built by the North British Locomotive Company in 1951 for deployment on the 1.68m (5ft 6in) gauge of the Indian Railways.

Interesting departures from previous Indian practice were the provision of greater firebox volume in relation to grate area by incorporating a large combustion chamber, one thermic syphon and two arch tubes and very massive box frames. The front end and the back end of the frames were each composed of a single steel casting. At the front this incorporated the buffer beam and drag box, and a similar casting was incorporated at the back end. There were also piston valves actuated by Walschaert's gear.

A batch of 50 WGs were the last steam locomotives to be built by Baldwin, but by far the majority of this huge class were built by Indian Railways' own plant at Chittaranjan.

Below: *a Class WG 2–8–2 as built by North British Locomotive Company; and* bottom, *No 9348 at Mathwa, December 1980*

CLASS 11 4–8–2

Country of origin: Angola
Railway: Benguela Railway (FCB)
Date: 1951
Length overall: 21.107m (69ft 3in)
Total weight: 134.091kg (295,000lb)
Cylinders: two 533 x 660mm (21 x 26in)
Driving wheels: 1.372m (4ft 6in)
Axle load: 13,182kg (29,000lb)
Fuel: 18.5m³ (650cu ft) wood
Grate area: 3.7m² (40sq ft)
Water: 22,700 litres (5,000 Imp gal/6,000 US gal)
Heating surface: 165m² (1,777sq ft)
Superheater: 39m² (420sq ft)
Steam pressure: 14.1kg/cm² (200psi)

Adhesive weight: 52,727kg (116,000lb)
Tractive force: 16,375kg (36,025lb)

This class of six 4–8–2 passenger locomotives was built by North British Locomotive Company of Glasgow. They were to meet a requirement for engines to haul trains of up to 508 tonnes (500 tons) up gradients of 1.25% (one in 80) that included curves of 90m (300ft) radius. The axle load was limited to 13.2 tonnes (13 tons). The result stipulated was achieved by basing the new class on the standard South African Railways (SAR) Class 19C/19D 4–8–2, and making a few

alterations which were necessary for the burning of wood.

A spark arrester was fitted to the smokebox and a Kylchap (Kylala-Chapelon) exhaust system was provided. The boiler was pitched at 178mm (7in) higher than on the SAR locomotive, thus providing the space for a larger ashpan for which drenching pipes were fitted.

The locomotive fleet was exceptionally well-equipped, and in addition it was well maintained; eventually these locomotives were converted to burning oil.

The Class 11 No 403 at Benguela, August 1973

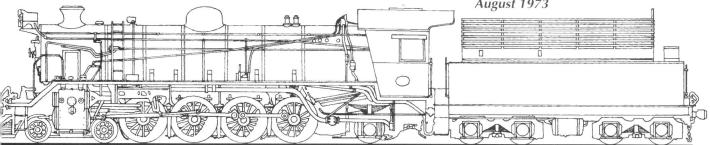

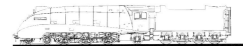

British Railways Standard Designs

CLASS 4 4–6–0

Country of origin: UK
Railway: British Railways (BR)
Date: 1952
Length overall: not known
Total weight: not known
Cylinders: two 457 x 711mm (18 x 28in)
Driving wheels: 1.727m (5ft 8in)
Axle load: not known
Fuel: not known
Grate area: 2.48m² (26.7sq ft)
Water: not known
Heating surface: 134m² (1,444sq ft)
Superheater: 24.62m² (265sq ft)
Steam pressure: 15.8kg/cm² (225psi)
Adhesive weight: not known
Tractive force: 11,383kg (25,100lb)

Class 4 No 75004 on the trestle at Dovey Junction with a down local, August 1964

The grouping of the railways in 1923 brought with it still further contraction and concentration on new design effort. At last with nationalisation in 1948, British Railways policy became vested in the single authority of the railway executive. Its aim in these twilight days of steam was to harness 120 years of development and produce a new range of standard locomotives that would be a synthesis of all that was best. Immediately a locomotive standards committee was set up, to consider the standardisation of design for the future and although some decisions were easy, others were not.

The decision to standardise on two cylinders was made for these reasons:
(1) to attain the ultimate in simplicity and accessibility for maintenance;
(2) because the split inside big end could be a source of trouble;
(3) a built-up crank axle is both expensive to build in the first place and expensive to maintain:
(4) four exhausts per revolution promote better steaming than either six or eight (ie from either three or four cylinders).

The main objectives were to achieve
(1) maximum steam-raising capacity;
(2) simplicity, with the least number of working parts and all of them to be readily visible and accessible;
(3) each new engine class to be so proportioned as to give the widest range of mixed-traffic working;
(4) a high standard of bearing performance;
(5) simplified preparation in the shed, by wide use of mechanical lubricators and grease lubrication;
(6) more rapid disposal by use of self-cleaning smokeboxes, rocking grates and self-emptying ashpans;
(7) high factors of adhesion to minimise slipping;

CLASS 5 4–6–0

Country of origin: UK
Railway: British Railways (BR)
Date: 1952
Length overall: not known
Total weight: 73,250kg (161,500lb)
Cylinders: two 483 x 711mm (19 x 28in)
Driving wheels: 1.88m (6ft 2in)
Axle load: 19,800kg (43,680lb)
Fuel: not known
Grate area: 2.7m² (28.65sq ft)
Water: not known
Heating surface: 153m² (1,650sc ft)
Superheater: 34.28m² (369sq ft)
Steam pressure: 15.8kg/cm² (225psi)
Adhesive weight: not known
Tractive force: 12,900kg (26,120lb)

Class 5 No 73015 embarks on a steady climb in 1956, under a fine exhaust

(8)   high thermal efficiency through large grate areas, a high degree of superheat and long lap gear.

Work began on seven British standard engine designs in 1949, with the work divided between the drawing offices of the old four main lines at Paddington, Derby, Doncaster and Swindon. The individual offices were each responsible not for an entire class, as might reasonably have been expected, but for the following components in respect of all engine types:

Brighton, brakes and sanding gear;
Derby, bogies and trucks; tenders, wheels, tyres, axles and spring gear;
Doncaster, coupling and connecting rods; valve gear and cylinder details;
Swindon, boiler and smokebox details; steam fittings.

The six classes for which work was undertaken initially were:

Class	Type
7 mixed traffic	4–6–2
6 mixed traffic	4–6–2
5 mixed traffic	4–6–0
4 mixed traffic	4–6–0
4P	2–6–4T
3P	2–6–2T

The boilers and fireboxes, in keeping with the design generally, were very simple in their conception. The narrow-firebox engines had boilers and fireboxes of the well-tried Swindon type, as modernised by Stanier in his latest London, Midland and Scottish (LMS) engines, while the Class 6 and 7 4–6–2 engines had straightforward wide fireboxes, without arch tubes or thermal syphons.

Four of the new classes, while incorporating to a major extent the standardisation design details and components, were largely adaptations of well-tried existing designs. For example, the new BR Class 5 mixed-traffic 4–6–0 was based on the Stanier Class 5 4–6–0 of

CLASS 6 (CLAN CLASS) 4–6–2

Country of origin: UK
Railway: British Railways (BR)
Date: 1952
Length overall: not known
Total weight: not known
Cylinders: two 495 x 711mm (19.5 x 28in)
Driving wheels: 1.88m (6ft 2in)
Axle load: 18,793kg (41,440lb)
Fuel: not known
Grate area: 3.34m² (36sq ft)
Water: not known
Heating surface: 193m² (2,073sq ft)
Superheater: 57.13m² (615sq ft)
Steam pressure: 15.8kg/cm² (225psi)
Adhesive weight: not known
Tractive force: 12,480kg (27,520lb)

Class 6 No 72002 **Clan Campbell**
*waits at Carlisle with a Glasgow to
Liverpool service, September 1960*

the LMS, which had been the largest class of modern locomotives in Britain. They had first been built in 1934, included several variations, and the class eventually numbered 842 engines.

The BR Class 4 2–6–4 tanks were similarly derived from LMS practice, while the Class 3 2–6–2 tank was derived from the Great Western Class 45xx 2–6–2 and the Class 4 4–6–0 was a lighter version of the Class 5.

However, it was the BR Class 7 that attracted the most attention and interest and after redesignation as the Britannia class eventually these locomotives gave sterling service, although initially they had encountered many troubles. The first 25 of the class to enter service were all withdrawn because of wheel problems and seven of these were declared failures, having shifting wheels. Once the wheel problem had been solved, the class proved to be one of excellent engines that were powerful and free-steaming, light on maintenance and well suited to the

prevailing conditions that the class had been designed to meet.

After the first six original British standard designs, the first examples of which had appeared in 1951–2, four other small types were introduced in 1953–4, all having the same family likeness and basic dimensions, as follows:
4MT 2–6–0 with 1.6m (5ft 3in) driving wheels and 444 x 660mm (17.5 x 26in) cylinders
3MT 2–6–0 with 1.6m (5ft 3in) driving wheels and 444 x 660mm (17.5 x 26in) cylinders
2MT 2–6–0 with 1.44m (5ft) driving wheels and 419 x 610mm (16.. x 24in) cylinders;
2MT 2–6–2T with 1.44m (5ft) driving wheels and 419 x 610mm (16.5 x 24in) cylinders

Of these, the 4MT series of 2–6–0s proved to be the most successful, quite able to undertake fast passenge working on fast cross-country routes with moderately laden trains.

CLASS 7 (BRITANNIA) 4–6–2

Country of origin: UK
Railway: British Railways (BR)
Date: 1951
Length overall: 20.9m (68ft 7in)
Total weight: 95,500kg (210,500lb)
Cylinders: two 508 x 711mm (20 x 28in)
Driving wheels: 1.88m (6ft 2in)
Axle load: 20,500kg (44,500lb)
Grate area: 3.9m² (41.98sq ft)
Heating surface: 229.83m² (2,474sq ft)
Superheater: 65.4m² (704sq ft)
Steam pressure: 17.5kg/cm² (250psi)
Adhesive weight: 61,700kg (153,740lb)
Tractive force: 14,600kg (32,100lb)

A total of 55 Britannia class locomotives were built between 1951 and 1953, and originally they were designated BR Class 7.

They were simple and rugged, with Belpaire fireboxes and roller bearings on all axles. They were the first full-size Pacifics on any British railway, with just two cylinders, and they were specifically designed to replace such renowned locomotives as the Royal Scot, Castle and West Country classes. They were the first of the new British Railways (BR) steam locomotive designs.

***The Class 7 No 70003** John Bunyan at Thetford, March 1962*

The Britannias were cheap and they were easy to maintain. British Railways allocated them to all regions, but the class made its reputation on the London to Norwich route, to which Eastern Region dedicated its fleet on a new high-speed service.

The first of the class was No 70039 *Britannia*, which having been built at the Crewe works appeared on 2 January 1951 in a dark green livery. It was capable of hauling 320-tonne (315-ton) trains at speeds of 105km/h (93mph), while at the same time showing a great economy of steam and having the capacity to produce some 1,641kW (2,200hp) in its cylinders.

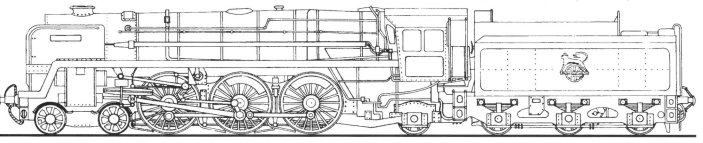

CLASS 8 4–6–2

Country of origin: UK
Railway: British Railways (BR)
Date: 1953
Length overall: 21.336m (70ft)
Total weight: 157,727kg (347,000lb)
Cylinders: three 457 x 711mm (18 x 28in)
Driving wheels: 1.88m (6ft 2in)
Axle load: 22,500kg (49,500lb)
Fuel: 10,000kg (22,000lb)
Grate area: 4.5m² (48.5sq ft)
Water: 19,635 litres (4,325 Imp gal/ 5,200 US gal)
Heating surface: 231m² (2,490sq ft)
Superheater: 64m² (691sq ft)
Steam pressure: 17.6kg/cm² (250psi)
Adhesive weight: 67,273kg (148,000lb)
Tractive force: 17,731kg (39,080lb)

The preserved No 71000 Duke of Gloucester *leaves Didcot, April 1990*

Permission to build a prototype for future British Railways (BR) top-line express passenger locomotives was granted in 1953. This class was to complement the Class 7 Britannias that had appeared in 1951.

This new class would have to have an extra cylinder, as if it was limited to just two the resultant cylinder size would be too large to clear the platform edges. British-Caprotti rotary-cam poppet valves were used on the prototype, No 71000 *Duke of Gloucester.*

This prototype showed on testing almost a 10% improvement over the Britannia class as regards the amount of steam consumed, achieving a world record for a simple (uncompounded) locomotive.

However, the *Duke of Gloucester* showed some signs of boiler problems in the production of economical steam at high outputs during this trial period.

The very purpose of a prototype is to resolve any problems encountered under testing, prior to ordering a production run. Yet, instead of investigating the problem in order to put right the fault, the authorities at BR took a different opportunity that it offered. Apparently they were determined that there should be no more development with steam, so nothing further was done and Class 8 remained a single-example class with a very short life before the engine was decommissioned.

CLASS 9F 2–10–0

Country of origin: UK
Railway: British Railways (BR)
Date: 1953
Length overall: 20.17m (62ft 2in)
Total weight: 88,000kg (194,040lb)
Cylinders: two 508 x 711mm (20 x 28in)
Driving wheels: 1.52m (5ft)
Axle load: 17,750kg (39,138lb)
Grate area: 3.73m² (40.15sq ft)
Heating surface: 187.1m² (2,014sq ft)
Superheater: 49.7m² (535sq ft)
Steam pressure: 17.5kg/cm² (250psi)
Adhesive weight: 79,700kg (175,400lb)

Right: a Class 9F with a Crosti boiler
Bottom:
*No 92099
ex-works
at South
Pelaw,
1966*

The standard BR Class 9 2–10–0 locomotives were remarkable engines, following on from the success of the Austerity class 2–10–0, and the last steam locomotives to be built for service on the home railways.

They had similar boilers to those of the Britannia class, but they were shorter, being 4.65m (15ft 3in) between the plates rather than 5.18m (17ft). As the locomotives were intended for mixed traffic as well as heavy-duty freights, the coupled wheels were designed to a 1.52m (5ft) diameter. This entailed the use of a shallower firebox than on the Pacifics, and a grate horizontal at the back and sloping in front. In addition, they were equipped with all the devices adopted to reduce maintenance and shed work, including rocker grates, hopper ashpans and self-cleaning smokeboxes.

British Railways had built ten of the standard Class 9F heavy freight variant 2–10–0s at Crewe works in 1955, with the Crosti type of boiler. This had been applied already in both Italy and Germany, to a number of locomotives. The idea of the Crosti was to pre-heat the water before it passed to the boiler, and thus increase thermal efficiency.

CLASS 25 4–8–4

Country of origin: South Africa
Railway: South African Railways (SAR)
Date: 1953
Length overall: 32.772m (107ft 6.25in)
Total weight: 238,636kg (525,000lb)
Cylinders: two 610 x 711mm (24 x 28in)
Driving wheels: 1.524m (5ft)
Axle load: 20,000kg (44,000lb)
Fuel: 19,091kg (42,000lb)
Grate area: 6.5m² (70sq ft)
Water: 19,976 litres (4,400 Imp gal/5,300 US gal)
Heating surface: 315m² (3,390sq ft)
Superheater: 58.5m² (630sq ft)
Steam pressure: 15.8kg/cm² (225psi)
Adhesive weight: 78,182kg (172,000lb)
Tractive force: 20,578kg (45,360lb)

South African Railways (SAR) had the intractable problem of having to traverse the Karoo Desert on the Cape Town to Johannesburg line, where it had to face the massive expense of supplying water for its locomotives. Hitherto it had hauled it in as well as having to maintain bore holes and pumps, but the Class 25 tender was designed to incorporate a condensing unit.

Previously many experimental condensing locomotives had been built, but condensing equipment is bulky and complex and any savings in fuel costs had been outweighed by higher maintenance costs. Henschel of Kassel, Germany, rebuilt 20 examples of a class of 2–10–2s as condensing locomotives following approaches from SAR. Success was

achieved by mounting the condenser on an extended tender, to which the exhaust steam was led before being reduced in temperature by large turbine-driven rotary fans. In this way the steam was condensed back to water for re-use in the boiler.

The results were promising, and SAR ordered a further 89 examples, not from Henschel but from North British Locomotive Company. It also ordered a further 50 non-condensing types, which were known as Class 25NC

In use the class proved to be very successful, leading to the closure of many of the expensive watering points and obviating the necessity to haul water to many others. With the advent of the diesel, the condenser types were converted to non-condensers.

The SAR Class 25 No 3503 at Deaar, July 1970

CLASS 01.¹⁰ 4–6–2

Country of origin: Germany
Railway: *Deutsche Bundesbahn* (DB, the German Federal Railway)
Date: 1953
Length overall: 24.13m (79ft 2in)
Total weight: 110,800kg (244,000lb) engine only
Cylinders: three 500 x 600mm (19.7 x 23.5in)
Driving wheels: 2m (6ft 6.7in)
Axle load: 22,200kg (44,500lb)
Fuel: 10,000kg (22,000lb)
Grate area: 3.96m² (42.6sq ft)
Water: 38,000 litres (8,400 Imp gal/10,000 US gal)
Heating surface: 206.5m² (2,223sq ft)
Superheater: 96.2m² (1,035sq ft)
Steam pressure: 16kg/cm² (227.6psi)
Adhesive weight: 60,400kg (133,000lb)
Tractive weight: 16,830kg (37,200lb)

The DB class 01.1055 at Balm with the Köln to Hamburg train, 1968

This was a stop-gap class of locomotives, intended to hold the fort before making good the physical devastation inflicted on the German railway during the Second World War combined with the partition of the country, and the full-scale electrification and dieselisation of the network. The former name, *Deutsche Reichsbahn* (DR, the German State Railway), was applied after the War to the German Democratic Republic, while the Federal Republic adopted the name *Deutsche Bundesbahn* (DB, the German Federal Railway).

New steam construction was then limited to mixed traffic and freight. Although two completely new passenger expresses were built, they appeared only in 1957, when electrification was carrying all before it. Meanwhile, there was a considerable programme of rebuilding and the first engines to receive upgrading were the 55 three-cylinder Class 01.¹⁰, which had originally been built in 1939.

Originally they had been streamlined but after five years of inactivity and heavy repair work they reappeared without casing.

They had new fireboxes and combination chambers, Heinl feedwater heaters, all-welded boilers with tapered barrels and new front end systems with larger chimneys. Before they were finally withdrawn in 1975, 34 of them were converted to burning oil.

In East Germany, DR also rebuilt existing Class 01 locomotives. Here the transfer to cleaner motive power was not so hurried, and thus the rebuilding programme for steam locomotives was more extensive with 35 rebuilds, designated 01.⁵, appearing between 1961 and 1965. They featured all-welded boilers and larger fire grates to burn inferior-quality coal. The cylinders were larger (600 x 660mm/23.5 x 26in) but the axle load, driving wheels and their total weight in working order were all as their 01.¹⁰ counterparts.

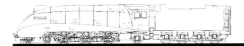

CLASS 59 4–8–2+2–8–4

Country of origin: Kenya
Railway: East African Railways (EAR)
Date: 1955
Length overall: 31.737m (104ft 1.5in)
Total weight: 256,364kg (564,000lb)
Cylinders: four 521 x 711mm (20.5 x 28in)
Driving wheels: 1.372m (4ft 6in)
Axle load: 21,364kg (47,000lb)
Fuel: 12,267 litres (2,700 Imp gal/ 3,250 US gal) oil
Grate area: 6.7m² (72sq ft)
Water: 39,044 litres (8,600 Imp gal/ 10,400 US gal)
Heating surface: 331m² (3,560sq ft)
Superheater: 69.4m² (747sq ft)
Steam pressure: 15.8kg/cm² (225psi)

Adhesive weight: 162,273kg (357,000lb)
Tractive force: 38,034kg (83,350lb)

These locomotives of Class 59, all 34 of which were built by Beyer, Peacock & Company, were the most powerful Garratt type to operate in South Africa. Moreover, thanks to the 21-tonne (20.7-ton) permitted axle load, they were the most powerful locomotives ever to be put on metre-gauge metals anywhere in the world. The power was commensurate with the work they were required to do.

They were designed to handle 1,219.2-tonne (1,200-ton) trains over grades of 1.5% (1 in 66) because that is the climb from Mombasa to Nairobi, up which every night the

legendary *Uganda Mail* made its way.

The locomotives were built on bar frames only 610mm (24in) apart, with all axles fitted with Timken roller bearings. Their big ends also incorporated roller bearings and they were fitted with Hadfield power-operated reversers. The class featured self-adjusting main pivots; streamlined ends to the two tanks; very long connecting rods driving on the third coupled axle and four sets of Walshaert's valve gear. All examples were fitted with Giesl ejectors by 1967.

They were the largest steam locomotives in use in the world by 1978, when 32 were still in service.

The EAR No. 5918 at Kibwezi, December 1972

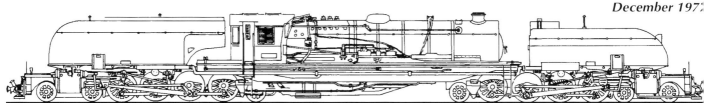

242F CLASS 4–8–4

Country of origin: Spain
Railway: *Rede Nacional de los Ferrocarriles Españoles* (RENFE)
Date: 1955
Length overall: 26.84m (88ft 0.75in)
Total weight: 213,000kg (459,500lb)
Cylinders: two 640 x 710mm (25.25 x 28in)
Driving wheels: 1.9m (6ft 2.72in)
Axle load: 19,000kg (42,000lb)
Fuel: 13,620 litres (3,000 Imp gal/3,600 US gal) oil
Grate area: 5.3m² (57sq ft)
Water: 28,173 litres (6,200 Imp gal/7,440 US gal)
Heating surface: 293m² (3,161sq ft)
Superheater: 104.5m² (1,125sq ft)
Steam pressure: 16kg/cm² (226psi)
Adhesive weight: 76,000kg 167,500lb)
Tractive force: 21,000kg (46,283lb)

The RENFE 242F class No 2005 at San Felices, 1969

Apart from the Prussian State Railways P.10 class, introduced in 1922, this was the only class of 4–8–4s ever to have been deployed in western Europe.

La Maquinista Terrestre y Maritima of Barcelona built this class of ten two-cylinder simple locomotives for the Spanish national railway system's 1.674m (5ft 5.9in) gauge, between 1955 and 1958. These examples belonged to the last European steam express passenger locomotive class, and represented an outstanding achievement by the Spanish locomotive engineers.

Lentz poppet valves were fitted to this class of oil-fired locomotives, together with a steam turbo-generator which provided electric current for lights on the locomotive as well as for lighting on the coaches of the train. They also had Walschaert's valve gear, which actuated an oscillating camshaft, a feed-water heater, a cab floor which was mounted on springs, and a Kylchap

(Kylala-Chapelon) double chimney.

The class was built for the purpose of hauling Spanish expresses from Madríd to the French border at Irún. Here trains often reached 762 tonnes (750 tons), although running speeds were low and they were required to maintain only 55km/h (35mph). When the locomotives were retired from these trains, they were employed on the Ávila to Miranda de Ebro trains.

One feature that worked against them was their small tenders. These were able to hold only 28,173 litres (6,200 Imp gal/7,440 US gal); this precluded the class from running long non-stop journeys, especially in the absence of water troughs.

The 242F class was the last class of steam passenger locomotive to be built and run in Europe, drawing to its conclusion a century of steam power. By opening up continents, this power had irrevocably changed the face of the world and the lives of its inhabitants. China continued to build steam

The names of individual locomotives, and the page numbers of illustrations, are shown in *italic* type; the page numbers of specifications appear in **bold**.

GENERAL INDEX

RM (PEOPLE) CLASS 4–6–2

locomotives at Datong, which is 270km (180 miles) west of Beijing, into the 1980s. These included both the Class JS (Jang Shan) 2–8–2s and the Class QJ (Quian Jin) 2–10–2s, of which about 300 were built specifically for freight haulage. Between 1985 and 1988 the plant also produced a new 4–8–4, which was based on the South African Railways 25NC type. Production ended at Datong in 1988.

The RM (Ren Ming) class 4–6–2s were built at the Szufung works. They were effectively an enlarged SL (Sheng-Li) class, but with the main

steam pipe running above the boiler in a well-insulated trucking. The locomotives each had two cylinders with outside-admission piston valves driven by Walschaert's valve gear, a wide firebox and a big superheater; they also had mechanical stokers.

Probably some 250 engines were built between 1958 and 1964. Their numbers run from RM1001, but there are a wide variety of insignia decorating the locomotives – and indeed all of the Chinese steam locomotives. These examples of the RM class must be regarded as the last design in the world of express passenger steam locomotives.

Country of origin: China
Railway: Railways of the People's Republic
Date: 1958
Length overall: 22.39m (73ft 5.5in)
Total weight: 174,000kg (384,349lb)
Cylinders: two 570 x 660mm (22.5 x 26in)
Driving wheels: 1.75m (5ft 9in)
Axle load: 21,000kg (46,284lb)
Fuel: 14,500kg (32,000lb)
Grate area: 5.75m² (62sq ft)
Water: 39,533 litres (8,700 Imp gal/ 10,400 US gal)
Heating surface: 210m² (2,260sq ft)
Superheater: 65m² (700sq ft)
Steam pressure: 15kg/cm² (213psi)
Adhesive weight: 62,500kg (137,750lb)
Tractive weight: 15,698kg (34,597lb)

PICTURE CREDITS

The illustrations in this publication are individually copyright and may not be reproduced in any form or by any means without the prior permission in writing of the copyright owners or their accredited agents. They are from the collection of ALDINO™, P O Box 207, Abingdon, Oxfordshire OX13 3TA, with the exception of the colour photographs that appear on pages 11 (bottom), 21, 23, 34 (top), 35–37, 39, 41–43, 47, 56–60, 63, 65–69, 71, 74–75, 78–80, 83–90, 93–101, 103–105, 107, 109–111, 113–114, 116–126, 128–141 and 144, which appear by permission of Colour-Rail, 5 Treacher's Close, Chesham, Buckinghamshire HP5 2HD, telephone 01494–78435&; the photographs that appear on pages 18 (bottom), 61, 62, 70, 73, 77, 102, 106, 108, 112 and 127 appear by permission of Millbrook House Limited, Calthorpe House, 30 Hagley Road, Birmingham, B16 8QY telephone 0121–454 1308.